Sindarin-English &
English-Sindarin L

First published May 2013
2nd Edition August 2014
3rd Edition June 2017

ISBN 978-1-291-33216-2

Acknowledgements and explanations

This dictionary originally started in 2012 from entries compiled from Hisweloke's Sindarin-English dictionary, without whose original work this project would have taken a lot longer to complete and I am grateful to the creator.

Words marked with a * have been deduced (attested only in compounds or other words).
Words marked with a † have been normalised or reconstructed from Noldorin.
All words marked with a ⅎ have been reconstructed by either myself or one of a number of other Tolkien enthusiasts and scholars throughout the world.
Words marked with a ● have been normalised from Goldogrin or Early Noldorin, which unfortunately makes them much more theoretical.

With exceptions for some irregulars, this dictionary does not contain plurals or verb parts other than the stem.

I have compiled the English-Sindarin dictionary to make life easier for students of Sindarin, however I advise you to cross-reference the Sindarin words back to their original glosses in the Sindarin-English to ensure the word means exactly what you want it to.

Second edition note: all entries have been changed so that the main entry is in the latest Sindarin form, with any earlier variants following it in brackets.

Third edition note: the text has been cleaned up to remove extraneous information, ease readability and solve spacing issues. All entries have been checked to ensure that they are still valid in modern Sindarin used in the Third Age onwards; this has resulted in around 100 entries being removed or modified and around 20 new entries.

Linguistic abbrevations

abst.	abstract
adj.	adjective
adv.	adverb
arch.	archaic
augm.	augmented
by ext.	by extension
card.	cardinal
conj.	conjunction
coll.	collective
dim.	diminutive
fem.	feminine
imp.	imperative
interj.	interjection
masc.	masculine
Mil.	military
n.	noun
N.	indicates an earlier variant of a word (Noldorin)
num.	number
ord.	ordinal
pl.	plural
poet.	poetic
pp.	past participle
pref.	prefix
prep.	preposition
pron.	pronoun
rel.	relative
sing.	singular
v.	verb

Other abbreviations

Ety	The Etymologies
EtyAC	Etymologies, Addenda and Corrigenda
GL	Gnomish Lexicon
LB	The Lays of Beleriand
Letters	The Letters of JRR Tolkien
LotR	The Lord of the Rings*
LR	Lost Road and other writings
LT	The Book of Lost Tales
LT2	The Book of Lost Tales, part 2
MR	Morgoth's Ring
PE	Parma Eldalamberon
PM	The Peoples of Middle-Earth
RC	The Lord of the Rings: A Reader's Companion
RGEO	The Road Goes Ever On
RS	Return of the Shadow
S	The Silmarillion
SA	Silmarillion Appendix
SD	Sauron Defeated
TAI	Tolkien: Artist and Illustrator
TT	Tyalië Tyelellièva
UT	Unfinished Tales
VT	Vinyar Tengwar
WJ	The War of the Jewels
WR	The War of the Ring

*Page numbers taken from the 50th Anniversary one volume edition

Sindarin-English

a I (**adh/ah/ar** before a vowel) *conj.* and (**ar** = Exilic, **ah** = Doriathrin, for **adh** see PE:17/41 for a discussion on this)

a II *interj.* O! See also **ai I**. RGEO/64

ab/ab- *prep.pref.* after, later. WJ/387

ꟻ **abarad** *n.* tomorrow 'after day'

ꟻ **abeneth** *n.* nickname, name given after birth 'after name'

ꟻ **abgen I** *n.* foresight, knowledge of what comes after 'after seeing'

ꟻ **abgen- II** *v.* to foresee, to know what comes after

ablad *n.* prohibition, refusal (with reference to the gesture one makes with the hand) VT:47/13

abonnen *pl.* **ebœnnin** *n. and adj.* **1.** born later, born after **2.** *as a noun*, man, one born later than the Elves, a human being. WJ/387

ach *prep.* but. VT:50/15

achad *n.* neck (properly referring only to the bony vertebral part not including the throat). PE/17:92

achar- *v.* to avenge. PE:17/166

acharn *n.* vengeance. WJ/254, WJ/301

***achas** *n.* dread, fear. This word may instead be **gachas**. WJ/187

ad- *adv.pref.* re-, back, again. PE/17:167

ada *n. masc.* daddy, dad *dim. of* **adar**. Ety/13

adab *n.* building, house. Ety/87

adan *n.* Man, the race of. PE/17:38, PM/324, WJ/387

***adanadar** *n.* man, one of the Fathers of Men. MR/373

adanath *n. class plural of* **adan**, all of the race of Men. MR/373

adaneth *n. fem.* (mortal) woman (of the race of Man) adan + -eth MR/323

adar *n. masc.* father PM/324, VT:44/22

ꟻ **adbanna-** *v.* to refill

adbed- *v.* to rephrase. PE/17:167

adel *prep.* behind, in rear (of). Ety/44

***adertha-** *v.* to reunite. S/113

ꟻ **adesta-** *v.* to rename

ꟻ **adforgam** *n.* ambidextrous 'double right-handed' (cf. Q. ataformaitë)

adh I *prep.* with, by

adh II *conj.* and, see **a**

†**adlann** (*N.* **adlant**) *adj.* sloping, tilted, oblique. EtyAC/26

†adlanna- *v.* to slope, slant. Ety/29, EtyAC/42

*adleg- *arch.poet.v.* to loose, let loose, release. EtyAC/14

adleitha- *v.* to release again, re-release. Ety/349, see also leithia-

adui *adv.* again. PE/17:167

aduial *n.* the evening, time of star-opening, 'evendim', second twilight. LotR/1111

advîr *n.* heirloom. PE/17:165

aear (*N.* gaear) *n.* sea. Letters/326, LotR/238, PE:17/27

aearon (*N.* gaearon) *n.augm.of* aear great sea, ocean. PE:17/27, RGEO/63,65

ꟻ aearvír *n.* pearl, 'sea jewel'

• aeborn *n.* cherry tree

*aeg *n.* point. PM/347

†aegas *pl.* †aegais *n. abst. of* aeg mountain peak. Ety/349

aeglir (*N.* oeglir) *n.* range of mountain peaks. RC/11

aeglos *n.* 1. snowthorn, a plant like furze (gorse), but larger and with white flowers 2. icicle. UT/99,148

†ael *pl.* aelin *n.* lake, pool, mere. Ety/10

aen *n.* conditional particle, changes the verb meaning to which it is attached to 'would/should'. VT/50:13

• aep *n.* cherry

aer *adj.* holy. VT/44:21,24

aerlinn *n.* a holy song, a song about the sea. RGEO/70

aes *n.* cooked food, meat. Ety/349

aew *n.* (small) bird. Ety/348, SA/6

*aewen *adj.* of birds. SA/6

*agar *n.* blood. S/210, see also iâr, sereg

agarwaen *adj.* bloodstained. S/210

aglar *n.* great glory, brilliance, splendor. RC/421, RGEO/63, SA/20, see also claur

aglareb *adj.* glorious. PE/17:24, SA/20, WJ/412

†aglonn *n.* defile, pass between high walls. Ety/348

agor *adj.* narrow. S/123

ah *prep. and conj.* and, see also a I

ai I *interj.* ah! hail! LotR/209, PE/17:16

ai II *pron. rel.* those who. VT/44:21

ꟻ aina- *v.* to hallow, bless (Q Aina-)

aith (*N.* eith) *n.* spearpoint. Ety/10

al- I *pref.arch.* no, not. see also **ú**. PE/17:100

al- II *adv.pref.* well. PE/17:146

alae *interj.* behold! UT/40

alaf (*N.* **lalf** *pl.* **lelf**) *n.* elm tree. Ety/348, PE/17:153

alag *adj.* rushing, impetuous. Ety/10

alagos *n.* storm of wind. Ety/13

albeth *n.* word of good omen. PE/17:146

• **alchor** *n.* temple, shrine

alfirin *n. and adj.* **1.** immortal **2.** *as a noun,* name of a flower, bell-like and running through many soft and gentle colours **3.** *as a noun,* used for another small white flower that looked like stars, also called **uilos**. PE/17:100, PE/22:153, UT/55

Ⅎ **alia-** *v.* cause to prosper, help someone, bless (Q. alya-)

alph *pl.* **eilph** *n.* swan. LoTR/1114, PE/17:100

alu *adj.* wholesome. PE/17:146

alwed *adj.* prosperous, fortunate. PE/17:146

am *prep.* up, upwards, upon. MR/320, PE/22:35

amar *n.* earth, the appointed home of Elves and Men. PE/17:105,124

amarth *n.* fate, doom. PE/17:104, PE/18:92, VT/41:10

amartha- *v.* to chance, destine, decree. PE/17:104

amarthan *adj.* fated. VT/41:10

amben (*N.* **ambenn, ambend**) *adj. and n.* **1.** *adj.* uphill, sloping upwards **2.** *n.* a difficult task (an uphill struggle). Ety/27

Ⅎ **amchalol** *adj.* uplifting

amdir *n.* hope based on reason, 'looking up'. MR/320

amloth *n.Mil.* flower or floreate device used as crest fixed to the point of a tall helmet, 'uprising flower'. WJ/318

amlug *n.* dragon. Ety/349, Ety/370

Ⅎ **ammad-** *v.* to devour (Q ammat-)

Ⅎ **ammal** *n.* flagstone (Q ambal)

Ⅎ **amman** *interrogative. pron.* why? ('for what?')

Ⅎ **ammas** *n.Mil.* breastplate

ammen *pron. 1st pl.* of us, for us, toward us. LotR/II:IV, LB/354, VT/44:21,27

Ⅎ **ammos** *n.* breast, bosom (Q ambos)

amon *n.* hill, steep-sided mount. Ety/348, LotR/E, RC/334

Ⅎ **amortha-** *v.* to heave, 'up-rise' (Q amorta-)

amrûn *n.* east, orient, 'uprising, sunrise'. Ety/348, Ety/384, S/437, LotR/E

an *prep.* to, towards, for. LotR/II:IV, UT/39, SD/129-31

an- *adv.pref.* with, by. Ety/374

anann *adv.* long, for a long time. LotR/VI:IV, Letters/308

anc *n.* jaw, row of teeth. Ety/348, Ety/374

and (*N.* **ann**) *adj.* long. Ety/348, S/427

andaith (*N.* **andeith**) *n.* long-mark, sign used in writing alphabetic tengwar over a vowel, to indicate that it is lengthened. LotR/E, Ety/391

†**andrann** (*N.* **anrand**) *n.* cycle, age (100 Valian Years, where 1 Valian year = 10 of our own, making this mean 'a millennium') Ety/382

andreth *n.* long-suffering, patience. PE/17:182

anfang *pl.* **enfeng** *n.* one of the Longbeards (a tribe of Dwarves) Ety/348, Ety/387, WJ/322

anfangrim *n.class pl.of* **anfang** the Longbeards (a tribe of Dwarves) WJ/322

ang *n.* iron. Ety/348, S/428, PM/347

angerthas *n.* runic alphabet, long rune-rows (extended version of the Certhas) S/427, LotR/E

***anglenna-** *v.* to approach. SD/129-31

angol *n.* deep lore, magic (perhaps also the subjects of science and philosophy, cf. Q. Ingolë). Ety/377

angren *adj.* of iron. Ety/348, S/428

angwedh *n.* chain, 'iron-bond'. Ety/397

anim *pron. 1ˢᵗ.* for/to myself. LotR/A(v), see also **enni**

aníra- *v.* to desire, to want. SD/129-31

ann-thennath *n. pl.* a verse mode, 'long-shorts' (alternance of long and short vowels, or rather alternance of long and short verse units, possibly of masculine and feminine rhymes). LotR/I:XI, Tolkien's Legendarium/115

***anna-** *v.* to give. Ety/348

annabon *n.* elephant, 'long-snouted'. Ety/372

annon *n. augm.* great door or gate. Ety/348, S/428, LotR/II:IV, TAI/150

annui *adj.* western. SD/129-31

annûn *n.* west, sunset. Ety/376, S/428, LotR/VI:IV, LotR/E, LB/354, Letters/308

annúnaid *n.* Westron, the language also known as Common Speech. PM/316

Anor *n.* sun. Ety/348, RC/232

ant *n.* gift. Ety/348

†**anu** (*N.* **anw**) *adj.* male. Ety/360

ᚠ **anuir** *adv. and n.* forever

anwar *n.* awe. UT/418, VT/42:23

aphada- *v.* to follow. WJ/387

aphadon *n.* **1.** follower **2.** *by ext.* man (elvish name for men). WJ/387

aphadrim *n.* *class pl. of* **aphadon** followers, men (elvish name for men). WJ/387

†**apharch** (*N.* **afarch**) *adj.* very dry, arid. VT/45:5

aphed- *v.* answer, reply. PE/17:166

âr *n.* king (used of a lord or king of a specified region) variant of the more commonly used **aran**

ar- *pref.* **1.** *arch.* beside **2.** *by ext.,* without. Ety/349

ara- *pref.* high, noble, royal. Reduced form of **aran**, element in the names of the kings of Arnor and Arthedain. S/428

arad *n.* daytime, a day. Ety/349

aran *n.* king (used of a lord or king of a specified region). Ety/360, S/428, LotR/II:IV, LotR/VI:VII, SD/129-31, Letters/426

Aran Einior *n.* one of the names given to the Vala Manwë, 'elder king'. PM/358

Aran Tauron *n.* one of the names given to the Vala Oromë, 'forester king'. PM/358

ᚠ **aranel** *n.* princess

aras *n.* deer. WJ/156-157

†**arasaith** *n.* avarice, excessive love of gold and gems and beautiful and costly things. SM/133

Araw *n.* one of the names given to the Vala Oromë. PE/17:138, WJ/400

arben (*N.* **arphen**) *n.* noble, knight. PE/17:147, WJ/376

ardh *n.* realm, region. Ety/360

ardhon *n.* *augm. of* **ardh** great region, province **2.** *by ext.* world. S/386, PM/348

ᚠ **arduil** *n.* early morning, 'day spring' (Q. aretuile)

aredhel *n.* noble Elf, one of the exiled Noldor. PE/17:139

ᚠ **aria-** *v.* to excel (Q arya-)

ᚠ **ariel** *n.* princess, king's daughter

ᚠ **arion** *n.* prince, king's son, heir

arnad *n.* kingdom. VT:44:21,25

arnediad (*N.* **arnœdiad**) *adj.* innumerable, countless, endless, without reckoning, numberless. Ety/349, Ety/378, S/428, VT/46:6

arnen *adj.* royal. LotR/V:I, WR/294, WR/370

arod *adj.* noble. PM/363, VT/41:9

ᚠ **arodas** *n.abst.of* **arod** nobility

aronoded *adj.* innumerable, countless, endless. Ety/378, see also **arnediad**

*__arwen__ *n. fem.* noble woman. LotR

Ⅎ __asg__ *n.* bone

__asgar__ *adj.* violent, rushing, impetuous. Ety/386

__ast I__ *n.* dust. Ety/349

__ast II__ *n.* light or heat of the sun. PE/17:18

__astor__ *n.* faith, loyalty. PE/17:183

__ath-__ I *prep.pref.* on both sides, across. Ety/349

__ath-__ II *adv.pref.* easily. PE/17:148

__athan__ *prep.* **1.** beyond **2.** preposition used in comparative sentences. SD/62

__atheg__ *n. masc. dim. of* __adar__, **1** play name for the thumb meaning 'little father' VT/48:6,17

__athelas__ *n.* 'kingsfoil', a healing herb brought to Middle-earth by the Númenóreans, 'healing leaf'. LotR/V:VIII, PE/22:166

__athgar__ *adj.* easy to do. PE/17:148

__athgen__ *adj.* easily seen. PE/17:148

__athon__ *pl.* __athof__ *v. affirmation* yes, I will *pl.* yes, we will. This is the only remaining part of the verb atha- PE/22:167

__athra-__ I *pref.* across. MR/329

__athra-__ II *v.* to cross (to and fro). PE/17:14

__athrabeth__ *n.* debate, converse, 'cross-talk'. MR/329

__athrad__ *n.* (river-)crossing, ford, way. Ety/349, Ety/383, UT/437, VT/42:7

*__athrada-__ *v.* to cross, traverse. Ety/383

*athragar- *v.* interact. PE/17:14

__athragardh__ *n.* interaction. PE/17:14

__aur__ *n.* a day, consisting of **calan** and **fuin, 2.** morning. Ety/349, S/439

✳__auth I__ *n.* war, battle. Ety/365, Ety/379, VT/45:23

__auth II__ *n.* a dim shape, spectral or vague apparition. VT/42:9

Ⅎ __authren__ *n.abst.of* __auth I__ war-like

__ava-__ *v.* to refuse, will not, do not. PE/17:143, WJ/371

__avad__ *n.* refusal, reluctance. PE/17:143, WJ/371

__avar__ *n.* **1.** refuser, **2.** the Avari, Elves who refused the invitation of the Valar. This plural name was known to the loremasters, but went out of daily use at the time of the Exile, see __gavar__ WJ/380, VT/47:12

__avo__ *v. imp. of* __ava-__, don't! Sometimes used as a prefix. WJ/371

*__avorn__ *adj.* staying, fast. SD/129-31

__avras__ *n.* precipice. PE/17:23

__awarth__ *n.* abandonment. Ety/397

awartha- *v.* to forsake, abandon. Ety/397

B

Ӿ **bá (mbá)** *n.* sheep (cf. Q. máma)

bach (mbach) *n.* article, thing, ware (*for exchange*) Ety/372

bachor (mbachor) *n.* pedlar. Ety/372

bâd *n.* beaten track, pathway. Ety/351

Ӿ **badh-** *v.* to judge

badhor *n.* judge. Ety/350, see also **badhron**

badhron *n. masc.* judge. Ety/350

baen *adj.* fair-haired. PE/17:155

Ӿ **bahad (mbahad)** *n.* market-place (bach+sad)

bain (*N.* **bein**) *adj.* beautiful, fair (due to lack of fault or blemish), wholesome, favourable. Ety/351, Ety/359

Ӿ **bainas** *abst.n.of* **bain** beauty

Ӿ **bal-** *v.* to rule, have power

Ӿ **Balagerch** *n.* the constellation known as the Sickle (Ursa Major)

balan *n.* Vala, divine power, divinity. Ety/350, S/439, Letters/427

balch (mbalch) *n. adj.* cruel. Ety/377

Ӿ **balchas (mbalchas)** *n.abst.of* **balch** cruelty

● **balfaug** *adj.* drunk (to be thirsty in a bad way). PE/13:138

balrog *n.* great demon, demon of might. PE/17:48

● **balthanc** *adj.* obstinate. PE/13:138

band (mband) (*N.* **bann**) *n.* duress, prison, custody, safe-keeping. Ety/371, S/428, MR/350

banga- (mbanga) *v.* to trade. Ety/372

Bannos *n.* one of the names given to the Vala Mandos 'dread imprisoner'. Ety/371

Banwen *n.* one of the names given to the Vala Vána. Ety/351

bar (mbar) *n.* **1.** dwelling, home **2.** *by ext.,* inhabited land. S/428, WR/379-80, SD/129-31

bara *adj.* **1.** fiery **2.** eager. Ety/351

barad (mbarad) I *adj.* doomed. Ety/372

barad II *n.* tower, fortress. Ety/351, S/428, LotR/B

baradh *adj.* steep. Ety/351

baran *adj.* brown, swart, dark brown, golden brown, yellow brown. Ety/351, LotR/F, TC/179, RC/343

bardor (mbardor) *n.* homeland, native land. PE/17:164

ᚠ **barn** *adj.* safe

***bartha-** (**mbartha**) *v.* to doom. Ety/372

barthan *n.* large stone building used as a dwelling. PE/17:109

basgorn (**mbasgorn**) *n.* loaf of bread, 'round bread'. Ety/372, Ety/365

***bass** (**mbass**, *N.* **bast**) *n.* bread. PM/404-405, VT/44:21

†**bassoneth** (**mbassoneth**) *n. fem.* bread-giver. PM/404-405

ᚠ **basta-** (**mbasta-**) *v.* to bake, cook

***batha-** *v.* to trample. Ety/352

baudh *n.* judgement. Ety/350

baug (**mbaug**) *adj.* tyrannous, cruel, oppressive. Ety/372

***baugla-** (**mbaugla**) *v.* to oppress. Ety/372

bauglir (**mbauglir**) *n.* tyrant, oppressor. Ety/372

baul (**mbaul**) *n.* torment. Ety/377

baur (**mbaur**) *n.* need. Ety/372

baw *interj.* no, don't! PE/17:143, WJ/371

bedhwen *adj.* 'of the spouses', referring only to Aulë and Yavanna together. Ety/369

belaith (**mbelaith**) *adj.* mighty. PE/17:115

beleg *adj.* big, large, great, mighty. Ety/352, S/428, PE/17:115

beleglinn (*N.* **beleglind**) *n.* Great Song. VT/50:5

Belegol *n.* one of the names given to the Vala Aulë, 'Great Aulë'. Ety/352

bellas *n.abst.of* **belt**, bodily strength. Ety/352

belt *adj.* strong in body. Ety/352, Tengwestie/20031207, see also **bellas**

ᚠ **beltha-** *v.* to expand

ben *prep.* according to the, as the. SD/129-31

benn *n. masc.* **1.** man, male **2.** *by ext.* husband (but not the normal word, see **herven**). Ety/352, VT/45:9

bennas *n.* angle, corner. Ety/352, Ety/375

beren *adj.* bold. Ety/352

ᚠ **berenas** *n.abst.of* **beren** courage, bravery

bereth *n. fem. and adj.* **1.** queen, spouse of a king, **2.** sublime, supreme. Ety/351, RGEO/74, see also **rîs**

***beria-** *v.* to protect. Ety/351

***bertha-** *v.* to dare. Ety/352

bess *n. fem.* **1.** (young) woman **2.** *by ext.* wife (but not the normal word, see **hervess**). Ety/352, SD/129-31

ᚠ best *n.* wedding, marriage

ᚠ besta- *v.* to wed, marry (bes+-tâ)

*blab- *v.* to beat, batter, flap (*wings, etc.*). Ety/380

ᚠ blabor *n.* bat 'flapper'

bo *prep.* on. VT/44:21,26

boda- *v.* to ban, prohibit. WJ/372

†boe (mboe, *N.* **bui)** *v. impers.* to need. This verb takes no other form. Ety/372

*bon (*N.* **bonn**) *adj.* snouted. Ety/372

bôr *n.* steadfast, trusty man, faithful vassal. Ety/353

Borgil *n.* 'hot red star', possibly Aldebaran. Letters/426-7

born *adj.* hot, red. Letters/426-27

● **bost** *n.* back (from shoulder to shoulder). PE/13:139

both (mboth)*n.* puddle, small pool. Ety/372

● **bothil (mbothil)** *n.* oven. PE/11:23

bragol *adj.* sudden. S/429

braig *adj.* wild, fierce. Ety/373, VT/45:34

brand I (*N.* **brann**) *adj.* **1.** lofty, noble, fine **2.** high (in size). Ety/351, PE/17:22, TAI/150

brand II *n.* steeple. PE:17/22

brannon *n. masc.* lord. Ety/351

brass I *n.* white heat. Ety/351

brass II *n.* great cliff. PE/17:23

brassen *adj.* white-hot. Ety/351

brasta- *v.* loom, tower up. PE/17:23

breged *n.* violence, suddenness. Ety/352

bregol *adj.* violent, sudden, fierce. Ety/352, Ety/373, see also **bregolas**

bregolas *n.abst.of* **bregol**, fierceness. Ety/352

*breitha- *v.* to break out suddenly. Ety/352

*brenia- *v.* to endure. Ety/353, VT/45:7

brennil *n. fem.* lady. Ety/351

breth *n.* acorns, nuts (mast – the fruit of beech, oak, chestnut and other woodland trees). EtyAC/13

brethil *n.* beech, beech-tree, silver birch. Ety/352, Ety/376, S/429

brith *n.* gravel. Ety/353

brôg *n.* bear. Ety/374, see also **graw, medli**

*brona- *v.* to last, to survive. Ety/353

16

bronadui *adj.* enduring, lasting. Ety/353

bronwe *n.* endurance, lasting quality, faith. Ety/353, SD/62

*****brui** *adj.* loud, noisy. LotR/Index

brûn *adj.* old, that has long endured, or been established, or in use. Ety/353

budhu *n.* large fly. PE/19:101

*****buia-** *v.* to serve, to hold allegiance to. Ety/353

bund (mbund, *N.* **bunn)** *n.* **1.** snout, nose **2.** *by ext.* cape (of land). Ety/372

†**bŷr** (*N.* **bior, beor**) *n.* follower, vassal. Ety/352

C

*cab- *v.* to leap. S/386, WJ/100

cabed *ger. of* cab-, **1.** leap **2.** *by ext.*, deep gorge. S/386, WJ/100

cabor *n.* frog. Ety/362

cad *prep.* after (when discussing time). PM/136

cadhad *n.* Dwarf. An old Beleriandic adaptation of the Dwarves' own name *khazad*. PE/17:45

cadhadrim *n. class pl. of* cadhad, Dwarf-folk. An old Beleriandic adaptation of the Dwarves' own name khazad. PE/17:45

†cadu (*N.* cadw) *adj.* shaped, formed. Ety/362-363

cadwor (*N.* cadwar) *adj.* shapely. Ety/363

†cae I (*N.* coe) *n.* earth. Ety/363

cae II (caen- in a compound) *adj. num. card.* ten. PE/17:95

ꝺ caeda- *v.* to lie down

cael *n.* lying in bed, sickness. Ety/363

caeleb *adj.* bedridden, sick. Ety/363

*caenen/caenui *adj. num. ord.* tenth. SD/129-131

ꝺ caenthil *n.* decagon 'ten points'

caer *n.* a flat isle in a river, opposite of a tol. PE/22:126

caew *n.* lair, resting-place. Ety/363

ꝺ caf- *v.* to bow

cáfru *n.* flea, 'leaper'. PE/13:140, PE/17:131

● cag *n.* joke. PE/11:24

cai *n.* hedge. UT/282

cail *n.* fence or palisade of spikes and sharp stakes. UT/282

cair (*N.* ceir) *n.* ship. Ety/365, LotR/A(iv)

calad *n.* light, radiance, glittering, reflection (from jewels, glass or polished metal, or water). VT/45:13, PM/347, Letters/425, Ety/362, UT/65

calan *n.* day, period of actual daylight. LotR/D, see also **aur, arad**

calar *n.* (portable) lamp. LotR/V:I, WR/287, RC/523

calardan *n.* lampwright. LotR/V:I, WR/287, RC/523

calben *n.* **1.** Elf of the Great Journey, 'light person' **2.** *by ext.* all Elves but the Avari. WJ/362, WJ/376-377, WJ/408-409

calen *adj.* green, 'bright-coloured'. Ety/362, S/429, Letters/282, RC/349, VT/42:19

callon *n.* hero. Ety/362

†**calph** (*N.* **calf**) *n.* water-vessel. Ety/362

ⴼ **calpha-** *v.* to draw water (Q calpa-)

cam *n.* hand. Ety/361, Ety/371, S/429

†**camlann** (*N.* **camland**) *n.* palm of hand. Ety/367, see also **plad, talf I**

ⴼ **camtha-** *v.* accommodate, make fit (Q camta-)

can- *v.* to cry out, shout, call. PM/361 362

canad *adj.num.card.* four. Ety/362, VT/42:24,25, VT/48:6, VT/46:3

canath *n.* silver coin used in Gondor, a quarter of a mirian. PM/45 see also **mirian**

†**cand** (*N.* **cann**) *adj.* bold. Ety/362

***cannas** *n.abst.of* **cant**, shaping. WJ/192, WJ/206

cant *n.* outline, shape. S/432, Ety/362, VT/42:28, see also **cannas**

ⴼ **canthil** *n.* quadrilateral 'four points'

canthui *adj.num.ord.* fourth. VT/42:10, VT/42:25,27

car (*N.* **cardh**) *n.* house, building. Ety/362

***car-** *v.* to do. WJ/371, WJ/415

carab *n.* hat. WJ/187

carach *n.* jaw, row of teeth. S/429, RC/607

***caraes** *n.* jagged hedge of spikes. Ety/362

carag *n.* spike, tooth of rock. Ety/362

ⴼ **caragpholg** *n.* boar (fang-pig)

caran *adj.* red. Ety/362, S/429, LotR/E

caras *n.* **1.** circular earthwall with dike **2.** city (built above ground). Ety/362, LotR/II:VII, RC/311

carch *n.* tooth, fang. Ety/362, S/429

ⴼ **carf** *n.* tool, weapon

carfa- *v.* to talk, speak, use tongue. PE/17:126

carth *n.* deed, feat. Ety/362

carweg *adj.* active, busy. PE/17:144

● **cas** *n.* skull. PE/13:140

***cast** *n.* cape, headland. VT/42:28

cathrae *n.* tressure, net for containing hair. VT/42:12

caul *n.* great burden, affliction. VT/39:10

caun I *n.* outcry, clamour. PM/361-362, see also **conath**

caun II *n.* valour. Ety/362

***caun III** *pl.* **conin** *n.* prince, ruler. LotR/VI:IV, Letters/308 ⱻ **cautha-** *v.* to startle

caw I *n.* top. Ety/362

caw- II *v.* to choose, taste, select. PE/22:152

ceber *n.* stake, spike, stone ridge. Ety/363, LotR/II:VIII, S/437, RC/327

cef *pl.* **ceif** *n.* soil. Ety/363

cefenas (*N.* **cefnas**) *n.* earthern-ware, pottery. EtyAC/12

● **ceforf** *n.* potato 'soil apple'. PE/11:42

†**celair** (*N.* **celeir**) *adj.* brilliant. Ety/362

celeb *n.* silver. Ety/367, S/429, LotR/E, Letters/426

celebren *adj.* like silver (in hue or worth). Ety/367, S/429, VT/45:25

celeg *adj.* swift, agile, hasty. Ety/366, PM/353, VT/41:10

celeth *n.* stream. EtyAC/15

celevon *adj.* of silver. Ety/367

ⱻ **celf** *n.* animal. This is less restrictive than **lavan**, and can apply to any living creature, see also **lavan**

*cell *adj.* **1.** running **2.** *by ext.* flowing (of water). LotR/Map

celon *n.* river that flows downwards from heights. Ety/363

†**celu** (*N.* **celw**) *n.* spring, source. Ety/363

†**cem** (*N.* **cefn**) *adj.* earthen. Ety/363

*cen- *v.* to see, perceive. PE/17:148

cenedril *n.* looking-glass, mirror 'looking crystal'. PE/17:37, RS/466, TI/184

cennan *n.* potter. Ety/390

cerch *n.* sickle. Ety/365

ceredir *n.masc.* doer, maker. Ety/354

ⱻ **cerf** *n.* spinning wheel

cerin *n.* **1.** circular enclosure **2.** *by ext.,* mound (Cerin Amroth). Ety/365, S/429

certh *pl.* **cirth** *n.* rune. LotR/E, WJ/396, see also **certhas**

certhas *n.abst.of* **certh** runic alphabet, rune-rows. LotR/E

cerveth (*N.* **cadloer**) *n.* July (month). LotR/D

ⱻ **cesta-** *v.* to seek (Q cesta-)

ceven *n.* Earth. VT/44:21,27

cidinn *adj.* small. PE/17:157

ⱻ **cil-** *v.* to choose

cîl I *n.* cleft, pass between hills, gorge. Ety/365

cîl II *n.* renewal. VT/48:8

cinnog *adj.* small. PE/17:157

cîr *adj.* renewed. VT/48:7-8

ⱡ **cira-** *v.* to sail

ⱡ **círam** *n.* anchor

†**círban** (*N.* **círbann**) *n.* haven. Ety/380

círdan (*N.* **cirdan**) *n.* shipbuilder, shipwright. Ety/365, Ety/390, LotR/VI:IX, RC/28

cirion *n.masc.* shipman, sailor. LoTR/1039

cirith *n.* cleft, high climbing pass, narrow passage cut through earth or rock, ravine, defile. S/387, UT/426, TC/181, RC/334-335

cîw *adj.* fresh, new. VT/48:7-8, see also **eden, gwain, sain**

claur *n.poet.* splendour, glory. Ety/362, see also **aglar**

côf *n.* bay. VT/42:15

cofen (*N.* **cofn**) *adj.* empty, void. Ety/366

ⱡ **col-** *v.* to carry, bear (Q. col-)

côl *n.* gold (the metal). Ety/365, see also **malt, mallen**

ⱡ **colch** *n.* box

coll I *adj.* red, scarlet, golden-red. Ety/365

coll II *adj.* hollow. WJ/414

coll III *n.* cloak, mantle. S/421, MR/385

● **colost** *n.* cucumber

conath *n.* *coll. of* **caun II, 1.** many voices **2.** *by ext.,* lamentation. PM/361-362

condir *n. masc.* mayor. SD/129-31

conui *adj.* commanding, ruling. LotR/A(ii)

corch *n.* crow. Ety/362

cordof *n.* pippin, small red apple. SD/129-31

cor *n.* ring. RC/625

corn *adj.* round, globed. Ety/365

coron *n.* **1.** globe, ball **2.** *by ext.* mound. Ety/365, S/429

†**coru** (*N.* **corw**) *adj.* cunning, wily. Ety/366

cost *n.* quarrel, dispute (not a quarrel of bolts). Ety/365

ⱡ **costha-** *v.* quarrel, dispute

● **cot** *n.* nut, seed. PE/11:26

coth *n.* **1.** enmity **2.** enemy. Ety/365

cova- *v.* to meet, to come together, gather, assemble. PE/17:158

covad- *v.* to make meet, to bring together. Transitive form of **cova-** PE/17:158

*__craban__ *n.* raven, type of large crow. LotR/II:III

__cram__ *n.* cake of compressed flour or meal (often containing honey and milk). Ety/365, LotR/II:VIII

__crann__ *adj.* ruddy (of face). Ety/362

● __crinth__ *adj.* pink. PE/11:27

__criss__ *n.* cleft, cut, slash. Ety/365, VT/45:23

__crissaegrim__ *n.* 'cleft mountain peaks', a mountain range south of Gondolin LR/301

__crist__ *n.Mil.* cleaver, sword. Ety/365

*__critha-__ *v.* to reap. Ety/365

__crom__ *n.* left. Ety/366

__crum__ *n.* left hand. Ety/366

__crumguru__ *adj.* guilty, sinister, wily (from the old meaning of 'sinister' referring to being left-handed). Ety/AC

__crumui__ *adj.* left-handed. Ety/366

__cû__ *n.* **1.** arch, crescent **2.***Mil.by ext.* bow. Ety/365, S/429

__cuen__ *n.* small gull, petrel, sea-bird. PE/22:32

__cugu__ *n.* dove. Ety/365

*__cuia-__ *v.* to live. LotR/VI:IV, Letters/308

__cuil__ *n.* life. Ety/366

__cuin__ *adj.* alive. Ety/366

*__cuina-__ *v.* to be alive. Ety/366

__cûl__ *n.* load. RC/536

Ɏ __culf__ *n.* orange (fruit)

Ɏ __culforn__ *n.* orange tree

Ɏ __cull__ *adj.* orange (colour)

__cum__ (*N.* __cumb__) *n.* mound, heap. Ety/365

__cûn__ *adj.* bowed, bow-shaped, bent. Ety/365

Ɏ __cúna-__ *v.* to bend, be bowed

†__cund__ (*N.* __cunn__) *n.arch.* prince. Ety/366, VT/45:24, see also __caun III__

● __cur__ *n.* cheese. PE/13:111

● __curtha-__ *v.* to turn milk. PE/11:28

†__cúron__ (*N.* __cúran__) *n.* the crescent Moon. Ety/365

__curu__ *n.* craft, skill. Applied to exceptional powers of mind or will, a skill not understood by the speaker. Does not apply to 'miracles' unless used by a Man. Ety/366, PE/22

curunír *n.masc.* man of craft, skill; wizard, Saruman. Ety/366, LotR/III:VIII, LotR/B, VT/45:24

*cyll *n.* bearer. MR/385

cýron *n.* new moon. VT/48:7

ꟻ **cytha-** *v.* to renew, refresh

D

dad *adv.* down, downwards. Ety/354

dadben (*N.* **dadbenn**) *adv.* **1.** downhill, inclined **2.** *by ext.* easy to achieve Ety/354, Ety/380, VT/46:8

ᚻ **dadhren-** *v.* to forget

dadwen- (**ndadwen-**) *v.* to return, go back. PE/17:166

dae (**ndae**) *n.* shadow. Ety/354, S/430

daebeth *n.* blasphemy. PE/17:151

daedelu *n.* canopy. Ety/391

daen (**ndaen**) *n.* corpse. Ety/375

daer I *adj.* great. UT/450, VT/42:11, WJ/187, WJ/335

†**daer II** (**ndaer**) (*N.* **doer**) *n.* bridegroom. Ety/375, VT/45:9

ᚻ **daetha-** *v.* to praise

ᚻ **daf-** *v.* to allow, permit

dâf *n.* permission. Ety/353

***dag-** (**ndag**) *v.* to slay. Ety/375, VT/45:37

dagnir (**ndagnir**) *n.* **1.** slayer **2.** *by ext.*, bane. S/430

dagor (**ndagor**) *n.* battle. Ety/375, S/430, see also **dagorath**

dagorath *n. coll. of* **dagor**, all the battles. UT/395-396

***dagra-** (**ndagra**) *v.* to battle. Ety/375

dam (**ndam**) *n.* hammer. Ety/375

damma- (**ndamma**) *v.* to hammer. Ety/375, VT/45:37

dan (**ndan**) *prep.* **1.** yet, against **2.** back. LotR/II:IV

ᚻ **dananna-** (**ndananna-**) *v.* to give back, return

dangar- *v.* to undo. PE/17:166

dangweth (**ndangweth**) *n.* answer, reply giving new information 'back report'. PM/395

ᚻ **danhir-** *v.* to lose

†**danna-** (*N.* **dant-**) *v.* to fall. Ety/354

dannen *n.* ebb, low tide. VT/48:26

dant *n.* fall. MR/373

danwaith (**ndanwaith**) *n.pl.* the Nandor (a group of Elves, once part of the Teleri, who turned back during the Great March). WJ/385

danwedh (**ndanwedh**) *n.* ransom. S/384

***dar-** *v.* to stay, wait, stop, remain. Ety/353

dartha- *v.* to wait, stay, last, endure, remain. Ety/353, VT/45:8

dath *n.* hole, pit, steep fall, abyss. Ety/354, VT/45:8

daug (ndaug) *n.* warrior, soldier (chiefly used of Orcs). Ety/375

daur *n.* **1.** pause, stop **2.** *by ext.,* league (about 3 miles). UT/279, UT/285

daw *n.* night-time, gloom. Ety/354

def- *v.* to try. PE/17:167

deil *adj.* delicate, beautiful and slender. PE/17:139,151

del *n.* fear, disgust, loathing, horror. Ety/355

deleb *adj.* horrible, abominable, loathsome. Ety/355

delia- *v.* to conceal. Ety/355

delos (*N.* **deloth**) *n.* abhorrence, detestation, loathing. Ety/355

†**delu** (*N.* **delw**) *adj.* hateful, deadly, fell. Ety/355

dem *adj.* sad, gloomy. Ety/354

dew- *v.* to fail, miss. PE/17:151

dha *adv.* there is (existential 'there'). PE/22:165

dî (ndî) *n.poet.fem.* bride, lady, *arch.* woman. Ety/352, Ety/354

di, di- *prep and pref.* beneath, under. LotR/IV:X, RGEO/72, Letters/278, VT/45:37

díhena- *v.* to forgive. VT/44:29, see also **gohena-**

dîl *n.* stopper, stopping, stuffing. Ety/354

dila- (ndila-) *v.* to be devoted to, love. PE/22:134

*****dilia-** *v.* to stop up. Ety/354, VT/45:9

dîn I *n.* silence. PE/17:95, S/430, LB/354

dîn II *n.* opening, gap, pass in mountains. Ety/354

dínen *adj.* silent. PE/17:98, S/430, WJ/194

dineth (ndineth) *n.* young bride. Ety/377-378, see also **dîs**

dîr (ndîr) *n.masc.arch.* man, referring to an adult male (elf, mortal, or of any other speaking race). Ety/352,354

dirbedui *adj.* difficult to pronounce. PE/17:154

dírnaith (nírnaith) *n.Mil.* a military wedge-formation launched over a short distance against an enemy massing but not yet arrayed, or against a defensive formation on open ground, 'man spearhead'. UT/282

dîs (ndîs) *n. fem.* bride. Ety/352, Ety/375, see also **dineth**

dofen (*N.* **dofn**) *adj.* gloomy. Ety/355

dôl *n.* **1.** head **2.** *by ext.* hill or mountain. Ety/376, S/430, RC/268

doll (ndoll) (*N.* **dolt**) *adj.* dark, dusky, obscure. Ety/355, Ety/376, Tengwestie/20031207

dolt *n.* round knob, boss. Ety/376

doltha- *v.* to conceal. Ety/355

dom *adj.* blind. PE/22:153

dond *n.* fist, hand. VT/47:23

donn *adj.* swart, swarthy. Ety/355

dôr (**ndôr**) *n.* land, dwelling-place, region where certain people live. Ety/376, S/430, WJ/413, Letters/417, VT/45:38, RC/384

dor-rodyn (*N.* **balannor**) *n.* Valinor, 'Land of the Ainur'. MR/200

dorn *adj.* stiff, tough. WJ/413

dornhabar *n.* Khazad-Dûm, 'Dwarrowdelf'. PE/17:35

dornhoth *n.class pl. of* **dorn** the Dwarves, 'the Thrawn Folk'. WJ/388

doron *pl.* **deren** *n.* oak tree. Ety/355, VT/45:11

****dortha-** (**ndortha**) *v.* to dwell, stay. Ety/376

†**dosta-** *v.* to burn. EtyAC

****drafa-** *v.* to hew. Ety/354, VT/45:8

drafen (*N.* **drafn**) *n.* hewn log. Ety/354

†**dram** *n.* heavy stroke, a blow (from an axe, etc.). Ety/354

drambor *n.* **1.** clenched fist **2.** *by ext.,* blow (with fist). Ety/354

draug *n.* wolf. Ety/354, S/430, see also **garaf**

ⱪ **drautha-** *v.* to tire, become weary

****drega-** *v.* to flee. UT/65

****dring** *n.* hammer. Ety/355, PE/17:84

****dringa-** *v.* to beat (with a hammer, etc.). Ety/355

drû *pl.* **drúin** *n.* wild man, Wose, Púkel-Man. UT/385

drúadan *pl.* **drúedain** *n.* wild man, one of the Woses. PE/17:99, UT/385

drúath *n. coll. of* **drû** the people of the Drû, the Woses. UT/385

drúnos *n.* a family of the Drû-folk. UT/385

drúwaith *n. class pl. of* **drû**, the wilderness of the Drû-men, the land inhabited by the Woses. UT/385

dû *n.* nightfall, late evening, night, dimness. Ety/354, S/430, VT/45:9

dúath *n. coll. of* **dû**, **1.** darkness, shadow **2.** nightshade. Ety/354, S/430

dufa- *v.* to lie heavy, be heavy, hang over oppressively (of clouds). Ety/AC

duin *n.* (long and large) river with a strong current. S/430, LotR/F, TC/179, VT/48:24

duinen *n.* flood, high tide. VT/48:26

duirro *n.* river-bank. VT/46:10

dúlinn *n.* nightingale, 'dusk singer'. Ety/354, Ety/369, S/430, see also **merilin**

dûn (**ndûn**) *n.* west. Ety/376, S/428, LotR/E-F

dúnadan (ndúnadan) *n.* Man of the west, Númenórean. LotR/I:XII, WJ/378, S/390

*****dúnedhel (ndúnedhel)** *n.* Elf of the West, Elf of Beleriand (including Noldor and Sindar). WJ/378

dûr *adj.* dark, somber. Ety/354, S/430, UT/434

ᚠ **durufuin** *n.* log night, Yule

dúven (ndúven) *adj.* sunken. EtyAC

dýgar *n.* **1.** mistaken act, **2.** *adj.* doing a wrong thing. PE/17:151

dŷl *n.* mistake. PE/17:151

dŷr *adj.* mistaken, off point, not right. PE/17:151

e *reflexive.pron.3rd* he/she/it. SD/129-31

*****eb** *prep.* before (when discussing time). PE/22:167

ech *n.* spine. Ety/355, VT/45:12

echad *n.* camp. UT/431

*****echad-** *v.* to fashion, make. Ety/363, LotR/II:IV

echil *n.* **1.** follower **2.** *by ext.* human being. WJ/219

echor *n.* outer circle, encircling, outer ring. LotR/V:I, LotR/Index, S/430

echui *n.* awakening. Ety/366, S/429

ƀ **echuia-** *v.* to awaken

echuir *n.* a season, the beginning of spring, 'stirring'. LotR/D, SD/129-31

ecthel *n.* point (of spear), 'thorn point'. Ety/388

ed, ed- *prep. and pref.* forth, out. Ety/356

edaid *adj. num.* double. VT/42:26-27

● **edeletha-** *v.* to deliver (from evil)

eden *adj.* new, begun again. Ety/349, see also **cîw, gwain, sain**

edhel *n.* Elf. Ety/356, S/430, WJ/363-364

edhelharn *n.* elf-stone. SD/128-129

edhellen *adj.* elvish, of the Elves. LotR/II:IV, RS/463

edhelvain *adj.* Elven-fair. PE/17:57

†**edinor** (*N.* **edinar**) *n.* anniversary day. Ety/400

†**edledhia-** (*N.* **egledhia-**) *v.* to go into exile. Ety/368, VT/45:27

†**edledhron** (*N.* **egledhron**) *n.* exile (person who is exiled). Ety/368

†**edlenn** (*N.* **eglenn**) *adj.* exiled. Ety/368

edlon *n.* outsider, stranger. PE/17:141

*****edlothia-** *v.* to blossom, flower. WR/293

edonna- *v.* to give birth. Ety/379

*****edra-** *v.* to open. LoTR/307, PE/17:45

†**edrain** (*N.* **edrein**) *n.* outside the border. Ety/383

edraith *n.* saving. LotR/II:IV, TI/175

edregol *adv.* in especial, especially. SD/129-31

edwen *adj. num. ord.* second. SD/129-31

êg *n.* thorn. Ety/355

*****egel** (*N.* **egl**) *n.* exile (one who is exiled). Ety/368

egladhrim *n. class pl. of* **eglan** 'The Forsaken', Elves of the Falathrim. WJ/189, WJ/365, WJ/379

eglan *n. and adj.* **1.** forsaken **2.** *as a noun,* an Elf of the Falathrim. WJ/365, WJ/379-380

eglath *n. coll. of* **egol** '(all of) The Forsaken', Elves of the Falathrim. WJ/189, WJ/344, see also **egladhrim**

****egleria-** *v.* to glorify, to praise. LotR/VI:IV, Letters/308

egnas *n.* **1.** sharp point **2.** *by ext.,* peak. VT/45:12

ego *interj.* be off! be gone! This is a strong insult. WJ/365

****egol** *n.* someone forsaken, an Elf of the Falathrim. WJ/189, WJ/344

egor *conj.* or. SD/129-31

ꝼ **eichia-** *v.* to change

****eil** *n.* sky. Ety/360

†**eiliant** *n.* rainbow, 'sky-bridge'. Ety/360, Ety/400, see also **ninniach**

einior *adj.* elder. PM/358

eirien *n.* daisy (flower). SD/129-31

eitha- *v.* **1.** to prick with a sharp point, to stab **2.***by ext.,* to treat with scorn, insult. WJ/365

eithel *n.* issue of water, spring, well, fountain. Ety/363, S/430, S/433, WJ/85, TC/187

eithro *adv.* also. VT/50:12

êl *pl.* **elin** *n.arch.poet.* star (little used except in verses). WJ/363, MR/373, RGEO/73, Letters/281, see also **elenath**

elanor *n.* a flower ('star sun'), a kind of enlarged pimpernel bearing golden and silver flowers. LotR/VI:IX, UT/432, Letters/402

elenath *n.coll.of* **êl**, starry host, all the host of the stars of heaven. LotR/II:I, RGEO/73-75, WJ/363

Elbereth *n.* one of the names given to the Vala Varda, 'star queen'. LoTR/378

†**elia-** *v.* to rain. Ety/396

ꝼ **ellen** *adj.* different, strange

elleth *n.fem.* elf-maid. WJ/148, WJ/256, WJ/363-364

ellon *n.masc.* elf. WJ/363-364

elloth *n.sing.of* **loth**, (single) flower. VT/42:18

elo *interj.* an exclamation of wonder, admiration, delight. WJ/362

†**elu** (*N.* **elw**) *adj.* (pale) blue. Ety/360

****elvellon** *n.* elf-friend. WJ/412

emel (*N.* **emil**) *n. fem.* mother. S/155, VT/48:17, see also **naneth**

emig *n.fem.dim. of* **emel**, play name for the index finger meaning 'little mother'. VT/48:6,17

emlin (*N.* **emmelin, emelin**) *n.* yellow bird, 'yellow hammer'. Ety/386

ꟻ **em** (*N.* **emm**) *n.* picture, image

ꟻ **elvennui** *adj.* wondrous, marvellous

en *art.* of the (genitival article). LotR/VI:IV, Letters/308

enchui (*arch.* **encui**) *adj. num. ord.* sixth. VT/42:10,25,28

ened (*N.* **enedh**) *n.* core, centre, middle. Ety/356, Ety/376, UT/450, Letters/224, VT/41:12,16

ꟻ **enedhinor** *n.* middle day of the year (in Gondorian reckoning, the 183rd day of the year) (Q. loëndë)

ꟻ **enedhor** *n.* noon

eneg *adj. num. card.* six. Ety/356, VT/42:25,31, VT/48:6,8

eneth *n.* name. VT/44:21,24

ꟻ **enethil** *n.* hexagon 'six points'

ꟻ **eng** *prep.* except, save

● **enn** *n.* mead

ꟻ **enna-** *v.* to exist in the universe as a creation of Eru

ennas *adv.* there, in that place. SD/129-31

enner *n.* one of the names given to the Vala Tulkas, 'bridegroom'. Ety/395

enni *pron. 1st* to me, for me. VT/41:11, see also **anim**

ennin *n.* Valian year, 'long year'. Ety/400

ennor (*N.* **emerin**) *n.* central land, middle-earth. LotR/E, see also **ennorath**

ennorath *n.coll.* of **ennor**, central lands, middle-earth. LotR/E, LotR/II:I, RGEO/72-75

eno *adv.* still. VT/50:17,19

ephel *n.* outer fence, encircling fence. S/436, LotR/E

ephola- *v.* to preserve, hold in memory, remember. VT/50:16

er *adj.* single. VT/48:6

er- *pref.* alone, one. VT/42:19

erch *n.* prickle. Ety/356

*****ercha-** *v.* to prick. Ety/356

erchamion (*N.* **erchammui**) *adj.* one-handed. Ety/361, WJ/51,231

†**erchammon** *n.masc.* one-handed man. VT/47:7

ereb *adj.* isolated, lonely. Ety/356, S/431, UT/422, VT/42:10

eredh *n.* seed, germ. Ety/356

ꟻ **eredhui** *n.* pea-pod, seed pod ('seed envelope', Q. orivaine)

ereg *n.* holly, thorn. Ety/356, S/431

eregdos *n.* holly, holly-tree. Ety/356, Ety/379, Ety/395

eregion *der.pl. of* **ereg** the land of holly. Ety/356, LotR, UT

*__eria-__ *v.* to rise. Ety/379, VT/46:7

erin *prep.* on the. SD/129-31

ernil *n.* prince. LotR/VI:IV, Letters/308, UT/428, RGEO/75

ero *adv.* alone. VT/50:18

*__ertha-__ *v.* to unite. S/409, see also **adertha**

eru *n.* waste, desert. Ety/356

erui *adj.* **1.** single, alone **2.** *by ext.,* first (incorrect use by the Gondorians). TI/312, WR/436, VT/42:10. The proper word for first in Sindarin was **minui**

ⱦ **Eruvan** *n.* Heaven (Q. Eruman, 'God + unmarred, blessed')

eryn *n.* wood. UT/436, LotR/B

esbin *n.* thin thread, tress. PE/17:17,119

esgal *n.* veil, screen, cover that hides. S/431

esgar *n.* shore. VT/46:14

*__esta-__ *v.* to name. SD/129-31

estel *n.* hope, trust, a temper of mind, steady fixed in purpose, and difficult to dissuade and unlikely to fall into despair or abandon its purpose. WJ/318-319, LotR/A(v), MR/320

ⱦ **estelia-** *v.* to trust

estent *adj.* very short. UT/146, WJ/311, WJ/315, see also **then, thent**

estolad *n.* encampment. UT/77, S/396

ⱦ **ethad-** *v.* to divide, share

ⱦ **ethel** *n.* foreign, outer lands

● **ethil** *n.* ivy. PE/11:33

ethir I *n.* mouth of a river, estuary, 'outflow'. LotR/II:X, Ety/356, RC/350

ethir II *n.* spy 'out watcher'. S/379, UT/418

ⱦ **ethiria-** *v.* to flow out

ⱦ **ethog-** *v.* to lead out

ⱦ **ethol-** *v.* to come forth

ethuil *n.* season of spring. LotR/D, SD/129-31

†**fadhu** (*N.* **fadhw**) *n.* parchment. PE/13:146

ⅎ **fadra-** *v.* to sate

fae *n.* a spirit dwelling within a body, the soul. MR/165

†**faeg** (*N.* **foeg**) *adj.* mean, poor, bad. Ety/387

fael I *adj.* fair minded, just, generous, 'having a good fëa'. PM/352

*fael II** *n.* gleaming brilliance (of the sun). LB/376, S/209-210

ⅎ **faelas** *n.abst.of* **fael I** justice, mercy, generosity

†**faen** (*N.* **foen**) *adj.* radiant, white. Ety/381

faer *n.* spirit (disembodied). MR/349

fain (*N.* **fein**) *n. and adj.* **1.** white **2.** *as a noun,* cloud. Ety/387, WR/288, RC/268, VT/46:15, see also **faun, fân**

†**fair** (*N.* **feir**) *n.* mortal. Ety/381, WJ/387

falas (*N.* **faur**) *n.* **1.** beach, wave-beaten shore, line of surf **2.**.*as a proper noun,* the western coast of Beleriand. Ety/381, S/431, RC/18

falathren *n.and adj.* **1.** of the shore **2.** *as a noun,* Shore-language (one of the names for Westron, or Common Speech). Ety/381, PM/32, PM/55

falathrim *n.class pl. of* **falas**, people of the Falas. WJ/378

*falch** *n.* deep cleft, ravine. UT/468

falf *n.* foam, breaker. Ety/381

faloth *n.* large foamy wave. PE/17:18

*faltha-** *v.* to foam. Ety/381

fân *n.* **1.** veil **2.** *by ext.,* cloud (applied to clouds floating as veils over the blue sky or the sun or moon, or resting on hills). PE/17:26, RGEO/74, see also **fain, faun**

fang *n.* beard. Ety/387

fanna- *v.* to veil, cloak, mantle. PE/17:174

ⅎ **fannil** *n.Mil.* staff

Fannor *n.* name given to the Fëanturi, Mandos and Lórien together. Ety/387

fanui *adj.* cloudy. RC/268, RGEO/74

Fanuilos *n.* one of the names given to the Vala Varda. PE/17:26, RGEO/63

fanwos *n.* mind-picture, vision (from a dream). PE/17:174

far *adj. or adv.* sufficient, enough, quite. Ety/381

*fara-** *v.* to hunt. Ety/387

faradrim *n. class pl. of* **feredir**, hunters. Ety/387

faras *n.abst.of* **fara-**, hunting. Ety/387

ꟻ **farf** *n.* carpet

farn *adj.* enough. Ety/381

***faron** *n.masc.* hunter. Ety/387

faroth *n.* hunter, group of hunters. S/431, Ety/387

fast *n.* shaggy hair. Ety/381

ꟻ **fasta-** *v.* to please

● **fath** *n.* tassel. PE/11:34

faug *adj.* thirsty. Ety/381

faun *n.* cloud. Ety/387, VT/46:15, see also **fain**, **fân**

***faw-** *v.* emit foul breath. PE/17:181

†**feir** *n.* right (hand). Ety/382, VT/46:10

feira- *v.* to suffice. VT/46:9

ꟻ **fel-** *v.* to feel emotion

fela *pl.* **fili** *n.* mine, boring, underground dwelling, cave. PE/17:118, Ety/381

ꟻ **felf** *n.* emotion, impulse

fen (*N.* **fenn**) *n.* door, threshold. Ety/381, LotR/V:IV, WR/341, RC/550, see also **fennas**

fennas *n.abst.of* **fen**, doorway, gateway. LotR/II:IV, RS/463, RGEO/75

fêr *pl.* **ferin** *n.* beech-tree. Ety/352, Ety/381

fergar *adj.* soon done. PE/17:181

fergenol *adj.* quick to see or perceive, sharp-sighted with the mind. PE/17:181

feria- *v.* to make ready. PE/17:181

feredir *n.* hunter. Ety/387

fern *n. and adj.* **1.** dead (of mortals) **2.** *as a noun,* dead person. Ety/381

ferui *adj.* ready to hand, quickly available. PE/17:181

fileg, filigod *n.* small bird. Ety/381

***fim** *adj.* slim, slender. LotR/Index

fîn (*N.* **find**) *n.* a single hair, filament. PM/361-362

fing *n.* lock of hair. RC/386

finnel (*N.* **findel**)*n.* (braided) hair. Ety/387

ꟻ **fion** *n.* hawk

***fir-** *v.* to die (for mortals). LotR/1107

fíreb *adj.* mortal. WJ/387

firen *n.* human. Ety/381

firiath *n. coll. of* **fair I**, mortals, human beings. WJ/219, WJ/387

fíriel *n. fem.* mortal maid. Ety/382, PM/195, PM/232

firieth *n. fem.* mortal woman. WJ/387

firion *n. masc.* mortal man. WJ/387

firith *n.* late autumn, season of fading. LotR/D

*****flâd** *n.* skin. LotR/E, TC/169, TC/173

ꝼ **fládvídh** *n.* sweat 'skin dew'

foen *n.* long sight (also a name given to a mountain in Beleriand). WJ/187

forgam *adj.* right-handed. Ety/382

forn *n.* right, north. Ety/382, UT/426, S/431

Forochel *n.* 'North Ice', an icy tundra region in the Northern Wastes where the Lossoth lived. LotR/1086

forod *n.* north. Ety/382, S/431, LotR/E, see also **forven**

forodren *adj.* northern. Ety/382

forodrim *n. class pl. of* **forod** Northmen. Ety/392

forodwaith (*N.* **forodweith**) *n.class pl. of* **forod**, **1.** Northmen **2.** *by ext.* the lands of the North. Ety/382, Ety/398

forven *n.* north. Ety/382, see also **forod**

forvo *n.* **1.** right hand **2.** *by ext.,* right side. VT/47:6

fû *n.* path. RC/526

*****fuia-** *v.* to feel disgust at, abhor. Ety/381

ꝼ **fuiol** *adj.* disgusting

fuin *n.* night, dead of night, gloom, darkness. Ety/354, Ety/382, S/431

• **fur-** *v.* to lie, to conceal the truth. PE/11:36

- **gach** *n.* milk cow. PE/11:36
- **gad-** *v.* to catch. Ety/358
- ₣ **gadas** *n.abst.of* **gad-** trap
- **gador** *n.* prison, dungeon. Ety/358
- ₣ **gadoras** *adj.* imprison, cage
- ₣ **gadorphen** *n.* prisoner
- **gae** *n.* dread. Ety/358
- **gael** *adj.* pale, glimmering. Ety/358
- **gaer I** *adj.* dreadful, awful, fearful. Ety/358
- †**gaer II** (*N.* **goer**) *adj.* red, copper-coloured, ruddy. Ety/358
- †**gaeruil** *n.* seaweed. PM/363, Ety/396, see also **uil**
- **gail** *n.* bright light. Ety/362
- **gais** *n.* steel. PE/11:37
- **gaithren** *adj.* of steel, steely
- **gaiw** *n.* pregnant. PE/11:37
- **gal-** *v.* to shine clear. PE/17:169
- *****gala-** *v.* to grow. Ety/357
- **galad** *n.* light, radiance, glittering, reflection (from jewels, glass or polished metal, or water). VT/45:13
- **galadh** *n.* large tree (such as oak and beech), thicker, denser and with more branches than a tree described as being an **orn.** Ety/357, S/427, LotR/E, LB/354, RGEO/73, Letters/426, see also **orn**
- *****galadhad** *n. dual pl. of* **galadh**, the Two Trees of Valinor. LotR/D
- *****galadhremmen** *adj.* tree-woven, tree-tangled. LotR/E, LotR/II:I, RGEO/72
- **galadhrim** *n.class pl. of* **galadh** Elves of Lothlórien, 'People of the trees'. Letters/426, LotR/341, PE/17:50
- **galas** *n.abst.of* **gala-**, growth, plant. Ety/357
- **galathil** *n.* one of the Two Trees of Valinor, known in Quenya as Telperion. UT/233, WJ/350
- **galenas** *n.* pipe-weed (leaf) or 'westmansweed', a variety of nicotiana (tobacco). LotR/V:VIII
- †**galu** (*N.* **galw**) *n.* blessings, blessedness, good fortune. Ety/357
- **galvorn** *n.* a black metal devised by the dark elf Eol. WJ/322-323, S/398
- **gammas** *n.abst.of* **gamp**, s-sign (special sign used to mark a final -s in Tengwar). VT/45:14
- **gamp** *n.* hook, claw, crook. Ety/357, VT/47:20

*__ganna-__ (__nganna__) *v.* to play a harp. Ety/377, see also __gannada-__

*__gannada-__ (__ngannada__) *v.* to play a harp. Ety/377, see also __ganna-__

__gannel__ (__ngannel__) (*N.* __gandel__) *n.* harp. Ety/377

*__gar-__ *v.* to hold, have. Ety/360

__garaf__ (__ngaraf__) *n.* wolf. Ety/377, see also __draug__

__gardh__ *n.* **1.** bounded or defined region. WJ/402

__garn__ *n.* 'own', property. Ety/360

__garth__ *n.* fort, fortress. Ety/360

Ⅎ __gartha-__ *v.* to defend

__gas__ *n.* hole, gap. Ety/357

__gasdil__ *n.* 'stopgap', name of a diacritic sign used to indicate that 'g' had been lenited to zero. Ety/354, Ety/357

__gath__ *n.* cavern. Ety/358

__gathrod__ *n.* cave. Ety/358, see also __fela__, __groth__

__gaud__ *n.* device, contrivance, machine. Ety/358

__gaul__ (__ngaul__) *n.* wolf-howl. Ety/377

__gaur__ (__ngaur__) *n.* werewolf 'false, disguised, deformed'. Ety/377, see also __gaurhoth__

__gaurhoth__ (__ngaurhoth__) *n. class pl. of* __gaur__, group of werewolves. LotR/II:IV

__gaurwaith__ (__ngaurwaith__) *n. class pl. of* __gaur__, wolf-men. UT/85, UT/90

__gavar__ *n.* an Avar, one of the Avari. PE/17:139

__gaw__ *n.* void. Ety/358

__gaw-__ (__ngaw__) *v.* to howl. Ety/377

Ⅎ __gawa-__ *v.* to disguise, falsify. PE/17:39

__geil__ (__ngeil__) *pl.* __gîl__ *n.* star, bright spark. Ety/358, PE/17:30, VT/45:15, see also __giliath__

Ⅎ __gelia-__ (__ngelia-__) *v.* to learn

__gelir__ *n.* merry, happy, gay person. SD/129-31

__gell__ *n.* joy, triumph. Ety/359

Ⅎ __gella-__ *v.* to rejoice

__gellam__ *n.* jubilation. Ety/359

__gellui__ *adj.* triumphant. Ety/359

Ⅎ __gellweg__ *adj.* joyful

__gem__ (*N.* __gemb__) *adj.* sickly. Ety/358

*__genedia-__ *v.* to reckon, count up. SD/129-31

__genediad__ *ger. of* __genedia-__, **1.** reckoning **2.** *by ext.,* calendar. SD/129-31

gern *adj.* worn, old, decrepit (used of things only). Ety/360

gildin *n.* silver spark. Ety/393

gilgalad (ngilgalad) *n.* starlight. Ety/358

giliath (ngiliath) *n. coll. of* **geil**, all the host of stars. Ety/358, RC/232

Gilthoniel *n.* one of the names given to the Vala Varda, 'star kindler'. Letters/278, RGEO/64

Ⴕ gilvír (ngilvír) (*N.* **élvír**) *n.* Mercury (the planet) 'star jewel'

*gir- *v.* to shudder. Ety/358

• **gîr** *n.* yesterday. PE/11:38

girith *n.* shuddering, horror. Ety/358, S/431

girithron *n.* December (month). LotR/D

glad *n.* wood. UT/452

gladh- *v.* to laugh. PM/359

glae *n.* grass. TT/17:33

glaer *n.* long lay, narrative poem. Ety/359, VT/45:15

glaew *n.* salve. Ety/369

glam (*N.* **glamm**) *n.* **1.** barbarous speech, shouting, confused noise **2.** din, uproar, the confused yelling and bellowing of beasts **3.** *by ext. as a coll. noun,* any body of Orcs. Ety/358, Ety/377, WJ/390, WJ/416

glamhoth *n. class pl. of* **glam**, barbaric host of Orcs, 'the dinhorde, the host of tumult'. Ety/358, Ety/364, Ety/377, UT/39, UT/54, WJ/390

glamog *n.sing.of* **glam** an Orc, 'a yelling one'. WJ/390

glamor (*N.* **glambr**) *n.* echo. Ety/358

glamren *adj.* echoing. Ety/358

*glân I *adj.* bright shining white. UT/390

glân II *n.* hem, border (of textile and other hand-made things). VT/42:8

Ⴕ glanas *n.abst.of* **glân I** purity, *by ext.* innocence

gland (*N.* **glann**) *n.* boundary. UT/264, UT/318, UT/441, VT/42:8

glandagol *n.* boundary mark. VT/42:8,28

glass *n.* joy. Ety/357

• **glast** *n.* marble. PE/11:39

glaur *n.* golden light (of the golden tree Laurelin). Ety/358, Ety/368

*glavra- *v.* to babble. Ety/358

glavrol *part. of* **glavra-**, babbling. Ety/358

glaw *n.* sunshine, radiance. Ety/362

glawar *n.* gold light, sunlight, radiance (of the golden tree Laurelin). Ety/368, VT/45:15

gleina- *v.* to bound, enclose, limit. VT/42:8, VT/42:28

glî *n.* honey. Ety/369

glim *n.* voice. PE/17:97

glîn (*N.* **glînn**) *n.* gleam, glint (usually of fine slender but bright shafts of light, particularly applied to light of eyes). WJ/337, S/431

Ⅎ **gling** *n.* music

glinga- *v.* to hang, dangle. Ety/359, Ety/369, VT/45:15,27

glinnel *n.* Elf, one of the Teleri, 'singer Elf'. WJ/378, WJ/385

glintha- *v.* to glance at. WJ/337

• **glinui** *n.* honey-bee

glîr *n.* song, poem, lay. Ety/359

glir- *v.* to sing, trill, to recite a poem. Ety/359, Ety/369, VT/45:15

***glirvaeron** *n.* songwriter 'maker of songs'. PE/17:163

Ⅎ **glist** *n.* sugar

gloss *adj.* snow-white, dazzling-white. Ety/359, RGEO/70, VT/42:18

Ⅎ **glosta-** *v.* to snow

glûdh *n.* soap. Ety/369

go- (*N.* **gwa-**) *pref.* together. Ety/399, WJ/367

gobel *n.* walled house or village, town. Ety/380

gobennas *n.* history. Ety/366

gobennathren *adj.* historical. Ety/366

Ⅎ **gobeth** (*N.* **gwabeth**) *n.* sentence, 'word collection'

gódhel *n.* Exiled Noldo, a 'Deep Elf' or 'Gnome', one of the Wise Folk. WJ/364, WJ/379, see also **gódhellim**

gódhellim *n. class pl. of* **gódhel** Exiled Noldor, 'Deep Elves' or 'Gnomes', the Wise Folk. WJ/364

†**godref** (*N.* **godrebh**) *adv.* through together. TAI/150

goe *n.* terror, great fear. PM/363

goeol *adj.* dreadful, terrifying. PM/363

Ⅎ **gofelf** *n.* sympathy, 'together emotion'

gohena- *v.* to forgive. VT/44:29, see also **dihena-**

golas *n.* foliage, collection of leaves. Letters/282, PE/17:84,159

golf *n.* branch (of a tree, or plant). Ety/359

goll (**ngoll**) *adj.* wise. Ety/377, see also **golwen, idhren**

gollor (**ngollor**) *n.* magician. Ety/377

golodh (**ngolodh**) *n.* sage, lore-master. In older Sindarin this referred to a Noldo. Ety/377, S/431, WJ/364

golodhbaeth *n.* Quenya, the speech of the Noldor. PE17/126

golodhrim (**ngolodhrim**) *n.class pl. of* **golodh** Noldor, 'Wise folk'. Ety/377, WJ/323

goloth (*N.* **gwaloth**) *n.* inflorescence, a head of small flowers. VT/42:18

golovir (**ngolovir**, *N.* **golodhvir**) *n.* Silmaril, 'Noldo-jewel'. Ety/373, see also **silevril, mirion**

Ⅎ **goltha-** (**ngoltha-**) *v.* to teach., see also **istanna-**

golwen (**ngolwen**) *adj.* wise, learned in deep arts. Ety/377, see also **goll, idhren**

gomaeron *n.* sculptor 'stone maker'. PE/17:163

gonathra- *v.* to entangle, enmesh. Ety/375

gonathras *n.abst of* **gonathra-**, entanglement. Ety/375

gond (*N.* **gonn**) *n.* great stone, rock. Ety/359, S/431

gondolindrim (*N.* **gondothrim**) *n.class.pl.* people of Gondolin. LT2/155

gondram (*N.* **gondrafn**) *n.* hewn stone. Ety/354

*gondren** *adj.* (made) of stone. TI/268,287

†**gonef** (*N.* **goneb**) *adj.* similar. PE/13:164

gonnhirim *n.class.pl.* Dwarves, 'masters of stone'. S/91

gonod- *v.* to count, count up, reckon, sum up. Ety/378, Ety/399, VT/46:6

Ⅎ **gonodvaeras** *n.* mathematics

Ⅎ **gor-** *v.* to warn, counsel

gorbedui *adj.* only to be said with horror or grief, lamentable to tell. PE/17:154

gordh *adj.* difficult, laborious. PE/17:154

gorf *n.* impetus, vigour. Ety/359

gorgor (**ngorgor**) *n.* extreme horror, terror, haunting fear. WJ/415, RC/334-335

gorn I *adj.* impetuous. Ety/359

gorn (**ngorn**) **II** *adj.* revered. PE/17:113

gorog (**ngorog**) *n.* horror. WJ/415

goroth (**ngoroth**) *n.* horror. Ety/377

gorth (**ngorth**) **I** *n.* horror. WJ/415

*gorth II** *n.* a dead person. Letters/417, RC/526

gorthad (**ngorthad**) *n.* barrow 'place of the dead'. LotR/A(iii), PM/194

gortheb (**ngortheb**) *adj.* horrible. WJ/415

*gorthrim** *n. class pl. of* **gorth II**, the dead. RC/526

gost *n.* dread. Ety/359

gosta- *v.* to fear exceedingly. Ety/359

gowest *n.* contract, compact, treaty. Ety/397,399

grau *adj.* dark in colour, swart. Ety/AC

graw *n.* bear (possibly dark in colour). VT/47:12, see also **brog**, **medli**

groga- *v.* to feel terror. WJ/415

grond *n.Mil. and adj.* 1. weighty, ponderous, 2. *as a noun.* club. Ety/384, PE:17/99

groth (**ngroth**) *n.* 1. cave, tunnel, large excavation 2. delving, underground dwelling. WJ/415, S/431, VT/46:12

gruin *adj.* ruddy. Ety/384

gruitha- *v.* to terrify. WJ/415

*****gûd** (**ngûd**) *n.* foe. WJ/256

gûl (**gûl**) *n.* 1. magic lore, long study (being used mostly of secret knowledge, especially such as possessed by artificers who made wonderful things) 2. *by ext.,* perverted or evil knowledge, sorcery, necromancy. Ety/377, S/432, MR/350, WJ/383

guldur (**nguldur**) *n.* black arts, dark sorcery. PE/17:125

gûr I *n.* heart (in the moral sense), counsel. VT/41:11,15, see also **hûn**

gûr (**ngûr**) **II** *n.* death. Ety/377, see also **gurth**

guren *n.* my heart. VT/41:11

Gurfannor *n.* one of the names given to the Vala Mandos. Ety/377

gurgof *n.* traitor. PE/22:155

gurth (**ngurth**, N. **guruth**) *n.* death. S/432, UT/39, UT/54 Ety/377, see also **gûr II**

*****guruthos** (**nguruthos**) *n.* the shadow of death, death-horror. Letters/278, LotR/IV:X, RGEO/72

gwa- *v.* to go. PE/17:148

†**gwachaedir** (N. **gwahaedir**) *n.* seeing-stone, palantír. PM/186

gwador *pl.* **gwedeir** *n.masc.* brother (especially used of those not brothers by blood, but sworn brothers or associates). Ety/394

*****gwaeda-** *v.* to enfold. VT/46:21

gwaedh *n.* bond, troth, compact, oath. Ety/397

gwael *n.* gull. WJ/418 see also **maen**, **mŷl**

gwân *adj.* fair and pale. PE/17:165, see also **bain**

*****gwaen** *adj.* stained. S/378

gwaeren *adj.* windy. VT/42:15

gwaeron *n.* March (month). LotR/D

gwaew *n.* wind (that can be seen moving objects). Ety/387

***gwain** *pl.* ***gwîn** *adj.* new. LotR/D, Ety/399, see also **cîw**, **eden**, **sain**

gwaith (*N.* **gweith**) *n.* **1.** manhood **2.** *by ext.*, man power, troop of able-bodied men, host, regiment, people **3.** *by ext.*, region, wilderness. Ety/398, VT/46:21

gwanath *n.* death (act of dying, not death as a state or abstract). Ety/397, see also **gwanu**

gwann *adj.* departed, dead. Ety/397

***gwanna-** *v.* to depart, fade, die (for Elves). Ety/397, see also **fir-**

gwanod *n.* tale, number. Ety/378

†**gwanu** (*N.* **gwanw**) *n.* death (act of dying, not death as a state or abstract). Ety/397, see also **gwanath**

gwanûn *n.* a pair of twins. WJ/367, see also **gwanunig**

gwanunig *n.sing. of* **gwanûn**, a twin (one of a pair of twins). WJ/367

gwanur *n.* kinsman, kinswoman. Ety/378, Ety/392, LotR/A(iv), VT/46:6

gwarth *n.* betrayer. Ety/397

gwass *n.* stain. Ety/397

gwastar *n.* hummock. Ety/388, Ety/399

gwath *n.* **1.** shade, shadow, dim light **2.** stain. Ety/397, S/432

***gwatha-** *v.* to soil, stain. Ety/397

gwathel *n. fem.* sister, associate. Ety/392

gwathra- *v.* to overshadow, dim, veil, obscure. VT/42:9

gwathren *adj.* shadowy, dim. S/432, VT/42:9

***gwathui** *adj.* shadowy. PM/330

gwathuirim *n.class pl. of* **gwathui** the Dunlendings, people of Dunland 'shadowy people'. PM/330

gwaun *n.* goose. Ety/397

gwaur *adj.* soiled, dirty. Ety/397

gwê *n.* living creature. PE/17:189

gwedh *n.* bond. Ety/397

***gwedh-** *v.* to bind. Ety/397

• **gwef** *n.* louse. PE/11:45

†**gwelu** (*N.* **gwelw**) *n.* air (as substance). Ety/398

gwelwen *n.* air, lower air (distinct from the upper air of the stars, or the outer). Ety/398

gwend I *n.* bond, friendship. Ety/397-398

gwend II (*N.* **gwenn**) *n. f.* maiden, virgin. Ety/398

gweneth *n.* virginity. Ety/398

gwenyn *n. pl.* twins. PM/353, PM/365, see also **gwanûn**

***gweria-** *v.* to betray, cheat. Ety/397

gwest *n.* oath. Ety/397

***gwesta-** *v.* to swear. Ety/397

gweth *n.* report. PM/395

gwî *n.* net, web ◇ Ety/398

†**gwîb** *n.* penis. PE/13:146

gwilith *n.* air (as a region). Ety/398

gwilwileth *n.* **1.** butterfly **2.** the constellation Cassiopeia. Ety/398

gwing *n.* **1.** spindrift, flying spray **2.** foam (properly a flying spume or spindrift blown off wavetops). Ety/398, PM/392

gwinig *n.dim.* 'little baby', play name of the little finger. VT/48:6,16-17

gwirith *n.* April (month). LotR/D, SD/129-31

● **gwista-** *v.* to be ignorant. PE/11:46

H

ha *pl.* **hain** *Doriathrin.pron.3rd* it. Ety/385, LotR/II:IV

hab- *v.* to clothe. Ety/363

habad *n.* shoe. Ety/386, VT/Errata

• **hach** *n.* hams, buttocks. PE/11:47

***had-** *v.* to hurl. Ety/363

hâdh *n.arch.poet.* cleaver. Ety/389

hadhod *n.* Dwarf. WJ/388, WJ/414

hadhodrim *n. class pl. of* **hadhod** the Dwarves (as a race). WJ/388

hadlath (*N.* **haglath**) *n.Mil.* sling. Ety/363, Ety/368

hador *n.Mil.* thrower (of spears and darts). Ety/363, WJ/234

hadron *n.masc.Mil.* thrower (of spears and darts). Ety/363

hae *adj.* very far away. PM/186, VT/45:21, PE/17:25

haedh *n.* fenced enclosure. PE/19:91

haer *adj.* remote. PE/17:25

Haerast *n.* the Far Shore, the east coast of Aman. PE/17:27

haered *n.* remote distance, the remote. LotR/II:I, RGEO/72

haeron *adj.* far, remote, distant. PM/273

haew *n.* custom, habit. Ety/364, VT/45:22

haf- *v.* to sit. VT/45:20

†**hair** (*N.* **heir**) *n. and adj.* left (hand). Ety/365

hâl *n.* small fish. VT/45:20, see also **lim III**

***hal-** *v.* to lift. VT/45:20

halethrim *n.class.pl* the people of Haleth, leader of the Haladin (one of the three Houses of the Edain). UT/140

half *n.* seashell. Ety/389

hall I *adj.* exalted, high. Ety/363

hall II *adj.* veiled, hidden, shadowed, shady. Ety/386

Ⅎ **hallas** *n.abst.of* **hall I** height

haltha- *v.* to screen. Ety/386

ham *n.* chair. VT/45:20

hamma- *v.* to clothe. Ety/363, VT/45:21

hammad *n.* clothing. Ety/363

hamp *n.* garment. Ety/363

hanar *n.masc.* brother. VT/47:14

hand (*N.* **hann**) *adj.* intelligent. Ety/363

ⱶ **hanna-** *v.* to thank

hannas *n. abst. of* **hand**, understanding, intelligence. Ety/363

ⱶ **hannweg** *adj.* thankful

harad *n.* south. Ety/365, S/432, LotR/E

haradren *adj.* southern. Ety/365

haradrim *n. class pl. of* **harad**, southerners, 'Southrons'. Letters/178, LotR/245

● **haran** *n.num.card.* one hundred (to the Gondorians)

hargam *adj.* left-handed. Ety/365

harn I *adj.* southern. Ety/365

harn II *adj.* wounded. Ety/386

harn III *n.Mil.* helmet. VT/45:21

***harna-** *v.* to wound. Ety/386

***hartha-** *v.* to hope. SD/62

†**haru** (*N.* **harw**) *n.* wound. Ety/386

harven *n.* south-region. Ety/AC

harvo *n.* **1.** left hand **2.** *by ext.,* left side. VT/47:6

hast *n.* axe-stroke. Ety/389

***hasta-** *v.* to hack through. Ety/389

hathol (*N.* **hathel**) *n.* **1.***Mil.* broadsword-blade, axe-blade **2.***Mil.by ext.* axe. Ety/389, WJ/234, UT/444, LR/433

haudh *n.* burial mound, grave, tomb. Ety/363-364, S/432, LotR/A(iv), see also **torn**

haust *n.* bed. Ety/364

he *pl.* **hîn** *Doriathrin.pron. 3rd. fem.* she. Ety/385

***heb-** *v.* to retain, keep, do not give away or release, keep hold of. VT/41:6

ⱶ **hedia-** *v.* to sneeze (*Q.* hotyo)

ⱶ **hel-** *v.* to freeze

helch *n.* bitter cold. Ety/364

heledh *n.* glass. S/433

heledir *n.* kingfisher (bird), 'fish-watcher'. Ety/363, Ety/386, Ety/394

heleg *n.* ice. Ety/364

ⱶ **helegren** *adj.* icy

heleth *n.* fur, fur-coat. Ety/386

helf *n.* fur. Ety/386

● **helin** *n.* pansy

● **helinil** *n.* violet

hell *adj.* naked. Ety/386, see also **lanc I**

ⅎ **Helluin** *n.* Sirius, a blue star

heltha- *v.* to strip. Ety/386, VT/46:14

hên I *pl.* **hîn** *n.* child. WJ/403

hen II *pl.* †**hin** *n.* eye. Ety/364, LotR/II:IX, WR/128, see also **hent**

*****heneb** *adj.* of eye, eyed, having eyes, 'sharp-eyed'. WJ/337

*****henia-** *v.* to understand. Ety/363

ⅎ **henna-** *v.* to read (silently, to oneself), see also **tengwa-**

henneth *n.* window. S/428

hent *n.dual pl. of* **hen II**, the two eyes (referring to one person's eyes). VT/45:22

ⅎ **her-** *v.* to pray

*****herdir** *n. masc.* master. SD/129-31

*****heria-** *v.* to begin suddenly and vigorously. Ety/364, VT/45:22

heron *n. masc.* master. VT/45:22

herth *n.Mil.* household, troop under a 'hír' (master, lord). Ety/364

herven (*N.* **hervenn**) *n. masc.* husband. Ety/352, Ety/364

herves (*N.* **hervess**) *n. fem.* wife. Ety/352, Ety/364

*****heryn** *n. fem.* lady. S/436

ⅎ **hest** *n.* captain

†**hethu** (*N.* **hethw**) *adj.* foggy, obscure, vague. Ety/364

*****hîl** *n.* heir. PM/369

him I *adj.* **1.** steadfast, abiding **2.***as an adverb,* continually. Ety/364

him II *adj.* cool. S/432

ⅎ **himannol** *adj.* continually harping, to speak about something repeatedly (Q vorongandelë)

ⅎ **himia-** *v.* to stick to, adhere to (Q. himya)

ⅎ **hir-** *v.* to find

hîr *n. masc.* master, lord. Ety/364, S/432, SD/129-31, Letters/382, LB/354, VT/45:22

hiril *n. fem.* lady. Ety/364

hîth (*N.* **hith**) *n.* mist, fog. Ety/364, S/432

hithlain *n.* mist-thread (a substance used by the Elves of Lothlórien to make strong ropes). LotR/II:VIII, LotR/Index

†**hithu** (*N.* **hithw**) *n.* fog. Ety/364

hithui *n. and adj.* **1.** foggy, misty **2.** *as a noun,* the month of November. LotR/D

hîw *adj.* sticky, viscous. Ety/364

ho *pl.* †**hyn** *Doriathrin pron. 3rd masc.* he. Ety/385

● **hô** *n.* owl

hobas *n. abst. of* **hûb** harbourage. Ety/364

****hol-** *v.* to close. PE/17:98, RC/550, see also **hollen**

hollen *pp.* closed. LotR/V:IV, RC/550

honeg *n.masc. dim.* 'little brother', play name given to the middle finger. VT/48:6,16-17

horn *adj.* driven under compulsion, impelled. Ety/364

hortha- *v.* to urge on, speed. Ety/364

host *n.* gross (144). Ety/364

hoth *n.* host, crowd, horde (nearly always in a bad sense). Ety/364, S/432

hû *n.* dog. Ety/364

hûb *n.* haven, harbour, small land-locked bay. Ety/364

hûd *n.* assembly. Ety/364

ⱶ **huia-** *v.* to urge on

● **huith** *n.* sex (intercourse)

hûl *n.* cry of encouragement in battle. Ety/386

hûn *n.* heart (physical). Ety/364, see also **gûr I**

ⱶ **hunna-** *v.* to thunder (Q. hunda)

huorn *n.* tree, with a spirit or heart. LoTR, PE/17:86

hûr *n.* readiness for action, vigour, fiery spirit. Ety/364

hwá *n.* breeze. PE/17:34

hwand (*N.* **chwann**) *n.* sponge, fungus. Ety/388

● **hwertha-** *v.* to sweep

†**hwest** (*N.* **chwest**) *n.* puff, breath, breeze. Ety/388

ⱶ **hwesta-** *v.* to puff (Q. hwesta-)

†**hwîn** (*N.* **chwîn**) *n.* giddiness, faintness. Ety/388

†**hwind** (*N.* **chwinn**) *adj.* twirling, whirling. Ety/388

hwinn *n.* birch. PE/17:23

†**hwinia-** *v.* to twirl, whirl, eddy. Ety/388

†**hwiniol** *part. of* **hwinia-**, whirling, giddy, fantastic. Ety/388

i *pl.* **in** *art. and pron. rel.* **1.** the **2.** who, that, which, whom. Ety/361, SD/129-31, Letters/308, Letters/417

iâ (*N.* **ia**) *n.* **1.** gulf **2.** abyss, void. Ety/400, S/432, Letters/383

*iach *n.* ford, crossing. S/286,382,387

iaeth *n.* neck. Ety/400

iaew *n.* mocking, scorn. Ety/400

ꟻ **iaf** *n.* fruit

ꟻ **iag-** *v.* to yawn, gape

ial *n.* a call, a cry. VT/46:22

ialla- *v.* to call (to someone), shout. VT/46:22

iant *n.* bridge. Ety/400, S/432

†**ianu** (*N.* **ianw**) *n.* yoke. Ety/400

iâr *n.* blood. Ety/400, see also **agar**, **sereg**

iarwain *n. and adj.* **1.** *n.* Elvish name of Tom Bombadil. **2.** *adj.* old-young (that is old, but yet still very vigorous) LotR/II:II, RC/128

ꟻ **ias** *conj.* where

iâth (*N.* **iath**) *n.* fence. S/433, WJ/370, WJ/378

iathrim *n.class pl. of* **iâth**, Elves of Doriath, 'people of the fence'. WJ/378

iau I *pl.* **iui** *n.* corn. Ety/399

iau II *n.* ravine, cleft, gulf. Ety/400, VT/46:22

ꟻ **iaul** *n.* cat

iaun *n.* holy place, fane, sanctuary. Ety/400

iaur *adj.* **1.** ancient, old, original **2.** older, former. Ety/358, Ety/399, S/433, UT/384

iavas (*N.* **dannas**) *n.abst of* **iau I**, season of autumn. LotR/D

íd *adv.* very, extremely (rarely used). PE/17:112

ꟻ **idh** *n.* small fly

îdh *n.* rest, repose. WJ/403

†**idhor** *n.* thoughtfulness. Ety/361

ꟻ **idhra-** *v.* to ponder

ídhra- *v.* to desire. PE/17:112

idhren *adj.* pondering, wise, thoughtful. Ety/361

†**idhrinn** (*N.* **idhrind**) *n.* year. Ety/383, Ety/400

• **idra-** *v.* to value, prize. PE/11:50

iell *n.fem.* **1.** daughter **2.** girl, maid. Ety/385, Ety/400

iest *n.* wish. Ety/400

Ⴕ **iesta-** *v.* to wish

îf *n.* cliff, sheer descent. PE/17:92

Ⴕ **iladar** *n.* Ilúvatar (GL ilador)

ilaurui *adj.* daily. VT/44:21,28

im I *imperative. reflexive. pron. 1st* I, myself. LotR/II:IV, LB/354, VT/47:14,37-38

im II (*N.* **imm, imb**) *n.arch.* dell, deep vale. This word only survives in compounds. VT/45:18, VT/47:14

im III *prep.* between. S/123

imlad *n.* deep valley, narrow valley with steep sides (but a flat habitable bottom). LotR/Index, RC/234,482, S/433, VT/45:18, VT/47:14

imladris *n.* Rivendell, 'cleft-valley', the home of Elrond. LotR

imloth *n.* flower-valley, flowery vale. This word only occurs in the place name Imloth Melui, a vale where roses grew. LotR/V:VIII, RC/582, VT/42:18

*imp *adj. num. card.* twelve. PE/17:95

imrad *n.* a path or pass (between mountains, hills or trackless forest). VT/47:14

imrath *n.* long narrow valley with a road or watercourse running through it lengthwise. RC/558, UT/465

Ⴕ **imu** *adj.* same, identical

în I *adj. poss. reflexive* own (referring to the subject). SD/129-31

în II *n.* year. Ety/40, see also **idhrinn**

inc *n.* guess, idea, notion. Ety/361

ind (*N.* **inn**) *n.* inner thought, meaning, heart. Ety/361, see also **innas**

Ⴕ **ing** *n.* imagination

Ⴕ **inga-** *v.* to guess

ingem *adj.* old (of person, in mortal sense: decrepit, suffering from old age), 'year sick'. Coined by the Elves after meeting Men. Ety/358, Ety/399, Ety/400

● **ingwil** *n.* eel

ínias *n.abst.of* **în II**, annals. Ety/400

Ⴕ **inil** *n.* lily

Ⴕ **inn** *n.* grandchild, descendant (Q. indyo)

innas *n.abst.of* **ind**, will. VT/44:21,26

†**inu** (*N.* **inw**) *adj.* female. Ety/361

io (*N.* **ia**) *adv.* ago. Ety/399

● **iol** *n.* lamb

48

*iôl *n.* wash, flood-water. RC/334, VT/48:33

iolf *n.* brand. Ety/400

ion (*N.* ionn) *n. masc.* **1.** son **2.***by ext.,* scion, male descendant. Ety/400, MR/373, PM/192,196

ionnath *n.coll.of* ion, all the sons. SD/129-31

†iphant (*N.* ifant) *adj.* aged, having lived long, old (with no connotation of weakness), 'year-full'. Ety/358, Ety/400, VT/46:23

ir *conj.* when/while. LB/354

îr *n.* sexual desire. VT/46:23

Ᵹ írui *adj.* desirable

ist *n.* lore, knowledge. Ety/361

*ista- *v.* to have knowledge. Ety/361, VT/45:18

Ᵹ istanna- *v.* to give knowledge, to teach, see also goltha-

istui *adj.* learned. Ety/361

ithil *n.* the (full) moon, 'The Sheen'. Ety/361, Ety/385, Ety/392, LotR/E, LB/354, RC/232

ithildin *n.* a silver-colored substance, which mirrors only starlight and moonlight. LotR/II:IV

ithron *n.* wizard. Letters/448, UT/448

iuith *n.* use. Ety/400

*iuitha- *v.* to employ, to use. Ety/400, VT/46:23

iûl *n.* embers. Ety/400

ivann *n.* a Sindarin form of the name of the Vala Yavanna, 'fruit giver'. PM/404

ivanneth *n.* September (month). LotR/D

*ivor *n.* crystal. LotR/A(v)

*ivren *adj.* of crystal, crystalline. S/392, WJ/85

L

*__laba-__ *v.* to hop. UT/60

● __laboth__ *n.* hare, rabbit

● __labum__ *n.* drum

†__lach__ (*N.* __lhach__) *n.* (leaping) flame. S/433

*__lacha-__ *v.* to flame

†__lachenn__ *n.* Noldo, 'flame-eyed'. WJ/384

__lad__ *n.* plain, valley. S/433

†__laden__ (*N.* __lhaden__) *adj.* open, cleared. Ety/368

†__lae__ (*N.* __lhae__) *n.* great number. VT/45:27

†__laeb__ (*N.* __lhoeb__) *adj.* fresh. Ety/368, VT/45:26

†__laeg I__ (*N.* __lhaeg__) *adj.* keen, sharp, acute. Ety/367, VT/45:25

__laeg II__ *adj.* 'viridis', fresh and green. Seldom used (replaced by __calen__). Letters/282,382

ⱴ __laegnas__ *n.abst.of* __laeg I__ sharpness, keenness

__laegel__ *n.* Green Elf, a Nando of Ossiriand. WJ/385

__laegrim__ *n. class pl. of* __laegel__, the Green Elves, the Nandor of Ossiriand. WJ/385

__laer I__ *n.* season of summer. LotR/D

__laer II__ (*N.* __lhaer__) *n.* song, long lay. S/406, VT/45:28

†__laes__ (*N.* __lhaes__) *n.* baby. Ety/367

†__laew__ (*N.* __lhaew__) *adj.* frequent, many. VT/45:27

†__lagor__ (*N.* __lhagr__) *pl.* †__legrin__ (*N.* __lhegrin__) *adj.* swift, rapid. Ety/367, VT/45:25, Tengwestie/20050318

__laich__ *n.* sweet to the taste. PE/17:148

†__lain I__ (*N.* __lhain__) *adj.* free, freed. Ety/368

*__lain II__ *n.* thread. LotR/II:VIII, LotR/Index

__lala-__ *v.* to laugh. PE/17:144

__lalaith__ *n.* laughter. S/406

†__lalorn__ *n.arch.* elm tree. Ety/367

__lalven__ *n.arch.* elm tree. Ety/348

†__lalwen__ (*N.* __lhalwen__) *n.arch.* elm tree. Ety/367

__lam I__ (*N.* __lham__) *n.* physical tongue. Ety/367, WJ/394

__lam II__ *n.* language or dialect of a particular country or people. WJ/394

__lamath__ *n.coll. of* __lam I__, echoing voices. PM/349

ⱴ __lamdaen__ *n.* consonant 'tongue-sign' (Q. lambetengwë)

__lamma-__ *v.* to echo. WJ/192

lammas *n. abst. of* **lam II**, account of tongues. LR/167, WJ/206, WJ/393

lammen *n.* my tongue. LotR/II:IV, PE/17:46

lanc I *adj.* naked. UT/418, see also **hell**

†**lanc II** (*N.* **lhanc**) *n.* throat. Ety/367

lanc III *n.* sharp edge (not of tools), sudden end (as a cliff-edge, or the clean edge of things made by hand or built). VT/42:8

†**land I** (*N.* **lhand**) *adj.* open space, level. Ety/368

land II (*N.* **lhann**) *adj.* wide, broad. LotR/VI:IV, Ety/367, see also **pann**

†**lang** (*N.* **lhang**) *n.Mil.* cutlass, sword. Ety/367

ꟻ **lann** *n.* tissue, cloth (Q lannë)

†**lant I** (*N.* **lhant**) *n.* clearing in forest. Ety/368

*ꟻ**lant II.** *n.* fall. S/406, PM/349

lanthir *n.* waterfall, 'falling river'. S/406, PM/349

● **lar** *n.* fat, grease

ꟻ **lar-** *v.* to hear

†**lasbelin** (*N.* **lhasbelin**) *n.* season of autumn 'leaf withering'. Ety/366-367

lass (*N.* **lhass**) *n.* leaf, especially those of trees; cannot apply to reed shaped leaves such as the hyacinth has. Ety/367, Letters/282, PE/17:62, TC/169

*ꟻ**lasta-** *v.* to listen. PE/17:46

†**lath** (*N.* **lhath**) *n.* thong of leather. Ety/368

ꟻ **latha-** *v.* to surpass (Q. lahta)

†**lathra-** (*N.* *lhathra-*) *v.* to listen in, eavesdrop. Ety/368

†**lathrada-** (*N.* **lhathrada-**) *v.* to listen in, eavesdrop. Ety/368

†**lathron** (*N.* **lhathron**) *n.* hearer, listener, eavesdropper. Ety/368

ꟻ **laub** *n.* shirt, tunic

laudh *n.* gluttonous eating. PE/19:92

†**laug** (*N.* **lhaug**) *adj.* warm. Ety/368

ꟻ **lausta-** *v.* to make a rushing, roaring noise (generally of wind)

†**lav-** (*N.* *lhaf-*) *v.* to lick. Ety/367

lavan *n.* animal (usually applied to four-footed beasts, and never to reptiles or birds). WJ/388, WJ/416, see also **celf**

†**laws** (*N.* **lhaws**) *n.* hair ringlet. Ety/370

le *pron. 2nd* thee (reverential). LotR/II:I, LotR/IV:X, RGEO/72-73, Letters/278, LB/354

lebdas *n.* index finger. VT/48:5

leben (*N.* **lheben**) *adj. num. card.* five. Ety/368, TAI/150, VT/42:24-25, VT/47:10, VT/47:24, VT/48:6

lebenedh *n.* middle finger. VT/48:5

lebent *n.* ring finger. VT/48:5

leber *n.* finger. VT/47:10,23-24, VT/48:5

lebethron *n.* a tree - a black Gondorian hard-wood (grown in Ithilien) that was used by the woodwrights of Gondor. LotR/IV:VII, LotR/VI:V, WR/176

lebig *n.dim.* little finger. VT/48:5,15, see also **niged**

ᚠ **lebthil** *n.* pentagon 'five points'

ᚠ **ledh-** *v.* to travel, journey

†**lefenar** (*N.* **lhevnar**) *n.* week (originally of five days). VT/45:27

legol *adj.* nimble, active, running free. Ety/368

leithia- (*N.* **lheithia-**) *v.* to release. Ety/368, see also **adleitha-**

leithian (*N.* **lheithian**) *n.* release, freeing, release from bondage. Ety/368, S/406

lembas *n.* waybread made by the Elves, 'journey bread'. PM/404, LotR/II:VIII

lemui (*N.* **lefnui**) *adj.num.ord.* fifth. WR/436, VT/42:25, TI/312

*****lend I** *n.* journey. PM/404

†**lend II** (*N.* **lhend**) *adj.* tuneful, sweet. Ety/369

ᚠ **lendren** *adv.* tunefully, sweetly.

lest *n.* girdle. WJ/225,228,333

†**lethril** (*N.* **lhethril**) *n. fem.* hearer, listener, eavesdropper. VT/45:26

leweg *n.* earth-worm. PE/17:160

†**lhaew** (*N.* **thlaew**) *adj.* sickly, sick, ill. Ety/386

†**lhain** (*N.* **thlein**) *adj.* lean, thin, meagre. Ety/386

lhaw *n.pl.* ears, pair of. Ety/368, LotR/II:IX, see also **lhewig**

†**lhê** (*N.* **thlê**) *n.* fine thread, spider filament. Ety/386

lhewig *n.sing. of* **lhaw**, ear. Ety/368, LotR/II:IX, see also **lhaw**

ᚠ **lhewigor** *n.* earring

†**lhind** (*N.* **thlinn**) *adj.* fine, slender. Ety/386

†**lhing** (*N.* **thling**) *n.* spider, spider's web, cobweb. Ety/386

†**lhingril** (*N.* **thlingril**) *n.* spider. Ety/386

†**lhîw** (*N.* **fliw**) *n.* sickness. Ety/386

lhoer *n.* venom. PE/17:185

lhoew *n.* poisonous substance. PE/17:185

lhôn *n.* sound, noise. PE/17:138

†**lhoss** (*N.* **thloss**) *n.* whisper or rustling sound. Ety/386

lhûg *n.* snake, serpent, reptile, worm. Ety/370, S/434

lhûn *adj.* full of water, applied particularly to rivers always full of water (that drained from the mountains). PE/17:137

ⅎ **lhussa-** *v.* to whisper (Q lussa-)

lî *n.* people (of one kind or origin). PE/17:190

***lif** *n.* link. VT/47:6

ⅎ **ligum** *n.* candle

ⅎ **lilth** *n.* dance

ⅎ **liltha-** *v.* to dance

lim I *adv.* quickly, swiftly. LotR/I:XII, PE/17:18

lim II *adj.* clear, sparkling, light. WJ/337

†**lim III** (*N.* lhim) *n.* large fish. Ety/369, see also **hâl**

†**limlug** (*N.* lhimlug) *n.* fish-dragon, sea-serpent. Ety/370

†**limmida-** (*N.* lhimmid-) *v.* to moisten. Ety/369

†**limp I** (*N.* lhimp) *adj.* wet. Ety/369

ⅎ **limp II** *n.* wine

ⅎ **limraedor** *n.* fisherman

lîn I *adj. poss. 2nd* thy, thine (reverential). VT/44:21,24

†**lîn II** (*N.* lhîn) *n.* pool. Ety/369

†**lind** (*N.* lhind, lhinn) *n.* air, tune. Ety/369

● **ling** *adj.* purple

● **lingui** *n.* hyacinth

***liniath** *n. coll. of* **lîn**, pools. WJ/194

***linna-** *v.* to sing. LotR/II:I

linnod *n.* a type of poem, perhaps a chant of a certain metrical type where each (half-)verse is composed of seven syllables. LotR/A(iv)

†**lîr** (*N.* lhîr) *n.* row, range. Ety/369

***liria-** *v.* to sing. VT/45:28, see also **linna-**

lisg *n.* reed, sedge. UT/34

liss *adj.* fragrant. UT/189

lith *n.* ash, sand, dust. Ety/369, S/434, TC/178

lithui *adj.* ashen, ashy, of ash, ash-coloured, dusty. S/434, UT/435, RGEO/74, TC/178, VT/42:10

lô *n.* shallow lake, fenland. UT/263, VT/42:8-10

lobor *n.* horse, for working. VT/45:28, see also **roch**

†**loch** (*N.* lhoch) *n.* ringlet. Ety/370

†**loda-** (*N.* lhoda-) *v.* to float. Ety/370

loeg *n.* pool. S/407, UT/450, LotR/Map

loen *adj.* soaking wet, swamped. VT/42:10

†**lom** (*N.* **lhom**) *adj.* weary. VT/45:29

lond (*N.* **lhonn**) *n.* **1.** narrow path or strait **2.** *by ext.,* entrance to harbour, land-locked haven. Ety/348, Ety/370, S/434, UT/450, VT/42:10

†**long** (*N.* **lhong**) *adj.* heavy. Ety/370

lonnath *n. coll. of* **lond**, havens. WR/294, WR/370

†**lorn** (*N.* **lhorn**) *n.* **1.** quiet water **2.** *by ext.,* anchorage, harbor. VT/45:29

loss *n.* snow. S/434, VT/42:18, RGEO/70

lossen *adj.* snowy. RGEO/70

Ⅎ **lossivor** *n.* snowflake 'snow-crystal'

Lossoth *n. class pl. of* **loss**, the people of Forochel, 'snowmen'. LotR/A, RGEO/70

†**lost** (*N.* **lhost**) *adj.* empty. Ety/370

Ⅎ **losta-** *v.* to sleep

loth (*N.* **lhoth**) *n.* flowers, inflorescence, a head of small flowers. Ety/370, LB/354, VT/42:18. The noun is collective, see also **lotheg**

lotheg (*N.* **lhothod**) *n.sing. of* **loth**, (single) flower. VT/42:18, see also **loth**

Ⅎ **lothlas** *n.* petal (flower-leaf)

lothron *n.* the month of May. LotR/D

†**lû** (*N.* **lhû**) *n.* a time, occasion. Ety/370

Ⅎ **lu** *n.* an hour (Q. **lúmë**)

Ⅎ **lúguil** *n.* lifetime

luin *adj.* blue. LotR (misc.), S/434, UT/390, Ety/370, VT/48:24

*luithia-** *v.* to quench. SD/62

● **lûl** *n.* sapphire

†**lum** (*N.* **lhum**) *n.* shade. Ety/370

†**lumren** (*N.* **lhumren**) *adj.* shady. Ety/370

†**lunt** (*N.* **lhunt**) *n.* boat. Ety/370

†**lûth** (*N.* **lhûth**) *n.* spell, charm. Ety/370

†**lútha-** (*N.* **lhútha-**) *v.* to enchant. Ety/370

lŷg *n.* snake. LotR/E

lytha- (*N.* **leutha-**) *v.* to pick up or out (with the fingers). VT/47:10,23

M

ma *interj.* good, excellent, that's right! PE/17:162

mâb *n.* a hand-full, complete hand (with all five fingers). Ety/371, VT/45:32, VT/47:6-7

ⱡ **maba-** *v.* to take, to grasp

ⱡ **mabed-** *v.* to ask (Q maquct-)

*mad- *v.* to eat. Ety/371

†**madh** (*N.* **madha**) *n.* mud. PE/19:101

madweg *adj.* gluttonous. PE/17:144

mae *adv.* well. LotR/I:XII, Letters/308

maecheneb *adj.* sharp-eyed. WJ/337

maed I *adj.* shapely. PM/366, VT/41:10

maed II (*N.* **moed**) *adj.* handy, skilled, skillful. Ety/371, VT/47:6

ⱡ **maeda-** *v.* to feed

maeg *adj.* sharp, piercing, penetrating, going deep in something. S/434, WJ/337

ⱡ **maega-** *v.* to knead, soften

mael I (*N.* **hmael**) *n. and adj.* 1. *n.* stain 2. *adj.* stained. Ety/386

mael II (*N.* **moel**) *n.* lust. Ety/373

maelui (*N.* **moelui**) *adj.* lustful. Ety/373

maen *adj.* skilled, clever. Ety/371

maenas *n.abst.of* **maen**, craft. Ety/371

maer *adj.* good, excellent, fair; useful, fit, good (of things). Ety/371

ⱡ **maeras** *n.abst.of* **maer**, goodness, usefulness

maeron *n.* artist, poet. PE/17:163

maeth *n.* battle, fight (not of general host but of two or a few). Ety/371

maetha- I *v.* to fight. Ety/371

maetha- II *v.* to handle, wield, manage, deal with. VT/47:6

maethor *n.* warrior. Ety/371

maew *n.* gull, 'whining bird'. Ety/373, see also **gwael**, **mŷl**

mâf *n.* pile or mass of rock or earth. PE/17:93

ⱡ **maga-** *v.* to forge metal (Q. maca)

magor *n.Mil.* swordsman. LotR/E, WJ/234

maidh (*N.* **meidh**) *adj.* pale, fallow, fawn. Ety/371

main *adj. num. ord.* prime, chief, pre-eminent. VT/42:10, VT/42:25

†**maitha-** *v.* to rape, ravish. PE/13:149

ᚠ **mal** *n.* moth (Q malo)

mâl *n.* pollen, yellow powder. Ety/386

malen *adj.* yellow. Ety/386

mallen (*N.* **malthen**) *adj.* of gold, golden. Ety/386, RC/625, VT/46:14, Tengwestie/20031207

● **maligon** *n.* amber

Mallorn *n.* golden tree of Lothlórien. S/435, LotR/II:IV, VT/42:27, Tengwestie/20031207

mallos *n.* a golden flower. UT/451, Letters/248

● **maloglin** *n.* daffodil. PE/11:56

malt *n.* gold (as metal). Ety/386, VT/46:14, VT/42:27, Tengwestie/20031207

†**malu** (*N.* **malw**) *adj.* fallow, pale. Ety/386

ᚠ **mammada-** *v.* to gorge, gobble up, devour. PE/22:95

man *interrogative. pron.* what?. TL/21:09

mân *n.* departed spirit. Ety/371

manadh *n.* **1.** doom, final end, fate, fortune **2.** *by ext.* final bliss. Ety/371

ᚠ **manen** *interrogative. pron.* how?

● **mang** *n.* butter

mann *n.* food. Ety/AC

ᚠ **mar** *interrogative pron.* when?

ᚠ **mas** *interrogative. pron.* where?

***matha-** *v.* to stroke, feel, handle. Ety/371

maur *n.* gloom. Ety/373

maw I *n.arch.* hand. VT/47:6

maw II (*N.* **hmaw**) *n.* soil, stain. Ety/386, VT/46:14

†**medli** (*N.* **megli**) *n..* bear, 'honey eater'. Ety/369, Ety/371, see also **brôg**, **graw**

†**medlin** (*N.* **meglin**) *adj.* honey-eater, bear-like. Ety/369

***medui** *adj.* end, final, last. LotR/I:XII, LotR/A(iv), PE/17:16

megil (*N.* **magol**) *n.Mil.* sword. Ety/371. PE/17:147

***megor** *adj.* sharp-pointed. WJ/337

mela- *v.* to love. VT/45:34, PE/22:134

melch *adj.* greedy. Ety/373

mêldir *n. masc.* friend. Ety/372

meldis *n. fem.* friend. Ety/372

meleth *n.* love. Ety/372

ᵮ **melethor** *n.* lover

melethril *n. fem.* lover. Ety/372

melethron *n. masc.* lover. Ety/372

mell *adj.* dear. Ety/372

mellon *n.* friend. Ety/372, Letters/424, LotR/II:IV, SD/129-31

• **melph** *n.* gooseberry

ᵮ **meltha-** *v.* to seduce

melui *adj.* lovely, sweet. LotR/V:VIII, VT/42:18, RC/582

men I *pron. 1st pl.* us. LotR/II:IV, LB/354, VT/45:37

men II *n.* way, road. UT/281

men- III *v.* to go, move, proceed in any direction (irrespective of speaker's position or point of thought). PE/17:93, PE/22:165

meneg *adj. num. card.* thousand. Given the Elven duodecimal system this properly means 1,728. S/409

menel *n.* sky, high heaven, firmament, the region of the stars. LotR/II:I, LotR/IV:X, LB/354, RGEO/72, VT/44:21,23-24

ᵮ **meneldaeg** *n.* horizon (menel+taeg)

Menelvagor *n.* the constellation of Orion, 'sky sword'. LotR/81, MR/456

*menniath** *n. coll. of* **ment**, **1.** many points **2.** *by ext.,* range of mountains. TI/124, Lambengolmor/799

ment *n.* point. Ety/373

ᵮ **mentha-** *v.* to send, cause to go

meren *adj.* festive, gay, joyous. Ety/372

mereth *n.* feast, festival. Ety/372, S/434

meril *n.* rose (flower). SD/129-31

merilin (*N.* **mœrilind**) *n.* nightingale. Ety/394, see also **dúlinn**

mesg (*N.* **mesc**) *adj.* wet. Ety/373

meth I *n. and adj.* end, last. Ety/373

*meth- II** *v.* end. UT/452

methed *n.* end. UT/452

methen *adj.* end, final. Ety/373, VT/45:34

• **miaug** *n.* tom, male cat

• **miaulin** *n.* queen, female cat

ᵮ **mib-** *v.* to kiss

mîdh *n.* dew. Ety/373

mîl *n.* love, affection. Ety/372

milbar *n.* dear home, place returned to after travelling, place of one's birth. PE/17:109,164

ⰲ **mill** *n.* oil (Q. millo)

milui *adj.* friendly, loving, kind. Ety/372

ⰲ **miluias** *n.abst.of* milui friendliness, kindliness

***mimp** *adj. num. card.* eleven. PE/17:95

min *prep.* in the, between (referring to a gap, space, barrier or anything intervening between two other things). LotR/Map, VT/47:11,14

mîn I *pron.poss. 1st pl.* our. VT/44:21,22,28

mîn II (*N.* min) *adj. num. card.* one (first of a series). Ety/373, VT/42:24-25, VT/48:6

ⰲ **mina** *prep.* into (mi+na)

†**minai** (*N.* minei) *adj.* single, distinct, unique. Ety/373

minas *n.abst.* **1.** tower **2.** *by ext.,* fort, city with a citadel and central watch-tower. Ety/373, S/434, VT/42:24

mindon *n.* **1.** isolated hill, especially a hill with a watch tower **2.** *by ext.* tower. Ety/373, Ety/395

minib *adj. num. card.* eleven. VT/48:6-8

miniel *n.* Vanyar, 'first Elf'. WJ/383

ⰲ **mininor** n. first day of the year (mîn+în+aur)

minlamad *n.* 'first voiced' or 'first-echoing', alliterative verse mode (minlamad thent/estent). The word is not translated by Tolkien but is likely to refer to the form and metre of *Beowulf* (lines of alliterative verse divided by a caesura). UT/146, WJ/311, WJ/315

ⰲ **minlû** *n.* once (one time)

minna- *v.* to enter, go in. LotR/305, PE/17:41

minui *adj. num. ord.* first. VT/42:10, VT/42:25

minuial *n.* 'morrowdim'; first twilight, the time near dawn when the stars fade. LotR/D

mîr *n.* jewel, precious thing, treasure. Ety/373, LotR/E, S/434, PM/348, LB/354, RGEO/73

***mírdan** *n.* jewel-smith. S/401

ⰲ **mírechor** *n.* bracelet.

míria- *v.* to sparkle like a jewel. PE/17:24

mirian *n.* piece of money, coin used in Gondor. PM/45

míriel *part.* sparkling like a jewel. RGEO/64, LotR/II:I

mirion *n. augm. of* **mîr** great jewel, Silmaril. Ety/373, see also **golovir, silevril**

miruvor *n.* 'precious juice', a special wine or cordial made by the Elves. LotR/290, PE/17:37

mist *n.* error, wandering. Ety/373

*__mista-__ *v.* to stray. Ety/373

†**mistad** *n.* straying, error. Ety/373

mith I *n.* white fog, wet mist. Ety/373

mith II *adj.* (pale) grey. Ety/373, S/434, TC/187

*__mithren__ *adj.* of grey. UT/436

mithril *n.* true-silver, a silver-like metal, 'grey brilliance'. LotR/317

mîw *adj.* small, tiny, frail. VT/45:35

moe *adj.* soft. Ety/371

moeas *n.abst.of* **moe**, dough. Ety/371

molif *n.* wrist, 'hand link'. VT/47:6

môr *n.* darkness, dark, night. Ety/373, Letters/382

morben *n.* Avar, one of the Avari. PE/17:141, WJ/376-377

morbenedh *n.* Avar, 'black speaker'. PE/17:140

*__morchant__ *n.* shadow (of objects, cast by light), dark shape. S/432, VT/42:9

morgul *n.* black arts, sorcery, necromancy, dark magic. Ety/377, S/432, WJ/383, MR/350, RC/482

morn *adj.* black, dark. Ety/373, Letters/382, Letters/427, WJ/368, WR/113, UT/65

mornedhel *n.* Dark-Elf, one of the Avari. WJ/377, WJ/380

*__muda-__ *v.* to labour, toil. Ety/373

ꟻ **mudathad** *n.* place of work, labour

ꟻ **muia-** *v.* to whine, complain

muil *n. and adj.* **1**. drear, **2**. dreariness. RC/334

muin *adj.* dear. Ety/374

muindor *n. masc.* dear brother. Ety/394

muinthel *n. fem.* dear sister. Ety/392

mûl *n.* slave, thrall. Ety/373

ꟻ **mulf** *n.* fine flour (Q. mulma)

ꟻ **mûn** *n.* womb (Q. móna)

mund *n.* bull. Letters/422-423

ꟻ **mûr** *n.* ink (Q. móro)

mŷl *n.* gull. WJ/379-380,418, see also **gwael, maew**

N

na I *prep.* with, by, of. Ety/374, LotR/I:XII, PE/17:147

na II *prep.* to, towards, at. PE/17:16,147

· ***na-*** *v.* to be. VT/44:21,24

nad *n.* thing. Ety/374

†nadh (*N.* **nadha**) *n.* fetter. PE/19:101

nadhor *n.* pasture. Ety/374

nadhras *n.abst.of* **nadhor**, pasture. Ety/374

nae *interj.* alas. Ety/375

naedh *n.* a wound, gash. PE/19:92

naeg *n.* pain. Ety/375

†naegra- *v.* to cause pain. Ety/375

†naer (*N.* **noer**) *adj.* sad, lamentable. Ety/375

Ⅎ naeras *n.abst.of* **naer** sadness

naergon *n.* woeful lament. PM/362

naeth *n.* woe; biting, gnashing of teeth in grief. Ety/374-375, WJ/258

naew *n.* jaw. Ety/374

nag- *v.* to bite. Ety/374

naglath *n. coll. of* **nagol**, the teeth. WR/122

***nagol** *n.* tooth. WR/122

nail (*N.* **neil**) *adj. num. ord.* third. VT/42:25

naith *pl.* **natsai** *n.* any formation or projection tapering to a point: a spearhead, triangle gore, wedge, narrow promontory. Ety/387, UT/282, RC/307

***nalla-** *v.* to cry. Letters/278, LotR/IV:X, RGEO/72

nan (*N.* **nann**) *n.* **1.** wide grassland, land at foot of hills with many streams **2.** *by ext.,* valley. Ety/374, S/435, Letters/308, VT/45:36

nana *n.dim.* mummy, mommy. Ety/348,374, see also **naneth**

naneth *n.* mother. Ety/348,374, see also **nana**

nâr *n.* rat. Ety/379

***nara-** *v.arch.poet.* to tell a story. Ety/374, VT/45:36

narbeleth *n.* October (month), 'sun-waning'. LotR/D

narch *adj.* bitter-biting. LotR, RC/601

narcha- *v.* to rend. Ety/374

nardh *n.* knot. Ety/387

narn *pl.* **nern** *n.* a tale or a saga, that is told in verse to be spoken and not sung. Ety/374, WJ/313, MR/373, S/412

*__narnvaeron__ *n.* author, maker of tales. PE/17:163

Ⰼ __narphen__ *n.* character of a story

*__nartha-__ *v.* to kindle. VT/45:37

*__narthan__ *n.* beacon, signal fire to notify of the approach of an enemy, 'fire sign'. VT/42:30

__naru__ (*N.* __narw__) *adj.* red. Ety/374

Ⰼ __naruvir__ *n.* ruby

__narwain__ *n.* the month of January 'new sun'. LotR/D

__nass__ *n.* __1.__ point, (sharp) end __2.__ angle or corner. Ety/375, VT/45:37

__nasta-__ *v.* to prick, point, stick, thrust. Ety/375, VT/45:37

__nath__ *n.* web. Ety/375

__natha-__ *v.* to help, save, rescue. PE/22:166

Ⰼ __nathaweg__ *adj.* helpful

__nathal__ *n.* guest. PE/17:141

Ⰼ __nathla-__ *v.* to welcome

*__nathra-__ *v.* to weave. Ety/375

__nathron__ *n.* weaver, webster. Ety/375

__naud__ *adj.* bound. Ety/378

__naug__ (*N.* __nawag__, *pl.* __neweig__) *n. and adj.* __1.__ stunted, dwarf __2.__ *.as a noun,* a Dwarf. Ety/375, WJ/388, UT/100, UT/148

__naugol__ (*N.* __naugl__) *pl.* __nauglin__ *n. dim. of* __naug__, dwarf. Ety/375

__naugrim__ *n. class pl. of* __naug__, Dwarves. WJ/388

__naur__ *n.* __1.__ flame __2.__ fire. Ety/374, S/435, LotR/II:IV

__nauth__ *n.* thought. Ety/378, VT/46:6

__nautha-__ *v.* to conceive. Ety/378

__naw__ *pl.* †__noe__ (*N. pl.* __nui__) *n.* idea. Ety/378

__nawb__ *n.* thumb. VT/48:5, see also __nobad__

__ned__ *prep.* in, during (with reference to time). SD/129-31,VT/47:40

__neder__ *adj. num. card.* nine. Ety/376, VT/42:25, VT/48:6, PE/17:95

Ⰼ __nederthil__ *n.* nonagon 'nine points'

__nedh-__ *pref.* in, inside, mid-. Ety/376

†__nedhu__ (*N.* __nedhw__) *n.* bolster, cushion. Ety/378

*__nedia-__ (*N.* __nœdia-__) *v.* to count. Ety/378, VT/46:6

__nedrui__ *adj. num. ord.* ninth. VT/42:25

__nef__ *prep.* on this side of. LotR/II:I, RGEO/72

__Nefrast__ *n.* 'Hither Shore', the westernmost coast of Middle-earth. PE/17:27

negen *adj.* angular, sharp. PE/17:55

*****neitha-** *v.* to wrong, to deprive. UT/456

neithan *adj.* deprived, wronged. UT/456

nêl (*N.* **neleg**) *pl.* **nelig** *n.* tooth. Ety/376, WR/113, VT/46:3

nelchaenen *adj. num. ord.* thirtieth. SD/129-131

neledh *adj. num. card.* three. Ety/376, TAI150, VT/48:6

*****neledh-** *v.* to enter. TAI/150

ꟻ **nelest** *n.* third (fraction)

ꟻ **nelf** *n.* needle

nell *n.* bell. Ety/379

nella- *v.* to sound (of bells). Ety/379, VT/46:7

nelladel *n.* ringing of bells. Ety/379

nelthil *n.* triangle. Ety/376, Ety/393

nelui *adj. num. ord.* third. VT/42:25

nem (*N.* **nemb**) *n.* nose. Ety/376

nen *pl.* **nîn** *n.* **1.** water (used of a lake, pool or lesser river) **2.** *by ext.* waterland. Ety/376, S/435, UT/457, RC/327-328

Nen Echui *n.* Cuiviénien, 'water of awakening', the lake by which the Elves first awoke. LR/406

nend (*N.* **nenn**) *adj.* watery. Ety/376

● **nenig** *n.* drop of water

ness *n.* headland. UT/28

*****nesta-** *v.* to heal. WR/379-380

*****nestadren** *adj.* healing. WR/380

*****nestag-** *v.* to insert, stick in. Ety/388

neth I *adj.* young. Ety/377

neth II *n. fem.* **1.** *from* **nîth** sister **2.** girl (in her teens, approaching adulthood). VT/47:14-16,33, VT/48:6

nethel (*N.* **thêl** *pl.* **thelei**) *n. fem.* sister. Ety/392, VT/47:14

nethig *n.fem.dim.* of **neth II**, 'little sister', play name given to the ring finger. VT/47:14, VT/47:38-39, VT/48:6,17

niben *adj.* **1.** small, petty **2.** *as a noun,* little finger (Elvish play-name used by and taught to children). S/435, WJ/388, WJ/408, VT/48:6

nîd *adj.* damp, wet, tearful. Ety/376

nîdh *n.* honeycomb. VT/45:38

nîdha- *v.* to be determined to (used when speaking of events in the future). PE/22:165

nîf *n.* front, face. Ety/378

niged *n.* little finger. VT/48:5, see also **lebig**

†nimmida- (*N.* **nimmid-**) *v.* to whiten. Ety/378

nimp I (*N.* **nim-**) *adj.* pale, white. Ety/378

nimp II *adj.* small and frail. VT/48:18

nin *pron.* me. LotR/IV:X, RGEO/72

nîn I *adj. poss. 1st* my. UT/40, VT/44:22

nîn II *n.* tear. Ety/376

nîn III *adj.* wet, watery. TC/195, S/435

†nind (*N.* **ninn**) *adj.* slender. Ety/378

ninglor *n.* golden water-flower, gladden. UT/280-81, UT/450

● **ningon** *n.* lapis lazuli

ᚠ **nínholch** *n.* onion 'tear-root'

ᚠ **nínia-** *v.* to weep

níniel *adj.* tearful. Ety/376

nínim *n.* snowdrop (flower) 'white tear'. Ety/367, see also **niphredil**

ninniach *n.* rainbow, 'water ford'. S/387, see also **eiliant**

nínui *n. and adj.* **1.** watery **2.** *as a noun,* the month of February. LotR/D

niphred (*N.* **nifred**) *n.* pallor, fear. Ety/378, S/435, see also **nínim**

niphredil (*N.* **nifredil**) *n.* a pale winter flower, snowdrop, 'pale point'. Ety/376, Ety/378, Letters/402, LotR/II:VI

nîr *n.* tear, weeping. Ety/376

nírnaeth *n.* (tearful) lamentation, weeping gnashing of teeth. Ety/376

ᚠ **niss** *n.* frost

nîth *n.* youth. Ety/377

ᚠ **nithren** *adj.* frosty

no *v. imp. of* **na-**, be! VT/44:21,24

nobad *n. dual pl. of* **nawb**, the pair of fingers composed of the thumb and the index (grouped together as in the act of picking something up). VT/48:5,16

†nod- *v.* to tie, bind. Ety/378

noen *adj.* wise, sensible. VT/46:9

ᚠ **nóf** *n.* mouth (including the lips)

nogoth *n.* Dwarf, 'one of the stunted folk'. S/435, WJ/338, WJ/388, WJ/408, WJ/413

nogotheg *n. dim. of* **nogoth**, 'dwarflet', a name of the Petty-Dwarves. WJ/388

nogothrim *n. class pl. of* **nogoth**, Dwarf-folk, 'stunted folk'. RGEO/75, UT/318, WJ/388

*****nor-** *v.* **1.** to run (of animals or men) **2.***by ext.,* to ride. PE/17:168

nordh *n.* cord. Ety/387

norn *adj.* **1.** twisted, knotted, crabbed, contorted **2.** hard. Ety/387

nornwaith *n. class pl. of* **norn** the Dwarves, 'hard folk'. MR/93, MR/106

noroth *n.* giant. Ety/AC

ᚠ **nor** *n.* murmur

north *n.* riding race. PE/17:168

northa- *v.* to make run, to race (on horses). PE/17:168

nórui *n. and adj.* **1.** sunny, fiery **2.** *as a noun,* the month of June. LotR/D

noss (*N.* **nos**) *n.* kindred, family, clan. Ety/378, PM/320

nost *n.* kindred, family, house. PM/360

ᚠ **nosta-** *v.* to smell (something)

nothlir *n.* family line (esp. as family tree, genealogical tree). WR/234, WR/237, WR/309

nothrim *n. class pl. of* **nost**, kindred, family, house. PM/360

ᚠ **novaer** *interj. and n.* farewell

nu *prep.* beneath, under. Ety/378, see also **nuin**

ᚠ **nui** *n.* bee

nuin *prep.* under the. Ety/378

nuitha- *v.* to stunt, to prevent from coming to completion, stop short, not allow to continue. WJ/413

ᚠ **nulaf-** *v.* to swallow 'down-lick'

nûr I *adj.* deep. Ety/378

nûr II *n.* race (of people). Ety/378

*****nûr III** *adj.* sad. UT/458, RC/457

†**nŷw** (*N.* **hnuif**) *n.* noose, snare. Ety/387

o **I** (**od**) *prep.* from, of (a place). Ety/360, WJ/366, WJ/369-70, LotR/II:IV, SD/129-31, RGEO/72, see also **uin**

o **II** *prep.* about, concerning. Ety/378

Ⅎ **ob** *prep.* before (when discussing space). PE/22:167

odhril *n. fem.* parent. Ety/379

odhron *n. masc.* parent. Ety/379

odog *adj. num. card.* seven. Ety/379, VT/42:25, VT/47:42, VT/48:6, PE/17:95

Ⅎ **odothil** *n.* heptagon 'seven points'

• **odrim** *adj.* many. PE/11:62

oer *adj.* nasty. PE/22:160

oew *n.* crime, evil deed. PE/17:170

ogol *adj.* wicked, evil. VT/48:32

ogron *n.* wicked or evil person. PE/17:170

ôl *pl.* **elei** *n.* dream. Ety/370, Ety/379

ola- *v.* to become, turn into (another state). PE/22:134

Olfannor *n.* one of the names given to the Vala Lórien, 'Lord of Dream-Cloud'. Ety/387

oll (*N.* **old**) *n.* torrent, mountain-stream. Ety/396

Ⅎ **olph** *n.* bottle

oltha- *v.* to dream. Ety/370, Ety/379

Ⅎ **ólui** *adj.* dreamy

****oneth** *n. fem.* giver. PM/404-05

ongol *n.* stench. Ety/378

****onna-** *v.* to beget. WJ/387

****onnen** *pp. of* **onna-**, born. WJ/387

• **onin** *n.* anvil

Ⅎ **onnor** *n.* parent, begetter

onod *n.* Ent. LotR/F, Letters/224

onodrim *n. class pl. of* **onod** the Ents, as a race. Letters/224, TC/165

or *prep.* above, over. Ety/379

or- *pref.* above, over. Ety/379

oraearon *n.* seventh day of the Númenórean week, Sea-day. LotR/D

oranor *n.* second day of the week, day of the Sun. LotR/D

orbelain *n.* sixth day of the week, day of the Powers or Valar. LotR/D

orch *n.* Goblin, Orc. Ety/379, LR/406, WJ/390, LotR/II:VI, LotR/F, Letters/178

orchal (*N.* **orchel**) *adj.* **1.** superior, lofty, eminent **2.** tall. Ety/363, Ety/379, WJ/305

orchoth *n. class pl. of* **orch**, the Orcs (as a race). WJ/390

Ⅎ **orf** *n.* apple

Ⅎ **orforn** *n.* apple tree

orgaladh *n.* fourth day of the Númenórean week, day of the Tree. LotR/D

orgaladhad *n.* fourth day of the Elvish week, day of the Two Trees. LotR/D

orgilion *n.* first day of the week, day of the Stars. LotR/D

orithil *n.* third day of the week, day of the Moon. LotR/D

ormenel *n.* fifth day of the week, Heavens' day. LotR/D

orn *n.* tree (such as ash or birch, not large trees). Ety/379, S/435, Letters/426, see also **galadh**

orod *pl.* **ered** (*N. pl.* **eryd**) *n.* mountain. Ety/379, S/435, Letters/263, TC/178, RC/621

orodben *n.* mountaineer, one living in the mountains. WJ/376

orodrim *n. class pl. of* **orod**, range of mountains. Ety/379

Ⅎ **oronnad** *n.* birthday ('begetting day', as Elves celebrate the conception not the birth)

oroth *n.* rage, anger. PE/17:183

***ortha-** *v.* to raise. Ety/379

***orthel-** *v.* to roof, screen above. Ety/391

orthelian *n.* canopy. Ety/391

***orthor-** *v.* to master, conquer. Ety/395

Ⅎ **órui** *adj.* daily, commonly, see also **ilaurui**

os- *pref.* about, around. Ety/379

***osgar-** *v.* to cut round, to amputate. Ety/379

osp *n.* reek, smoke. Ety/396

● **ospa-** *v.* to smoke

ost *n.* **1.** city, town with wall round **2.** citadel, fortress or stronghold, made or strengthened by art. Ety/379, S/435, WJ/414, RC/232

othgar- *v.* to do wrong. PE/17:151

othgarn *n.* misdeed. PE/17:151

†**othlonn** (*N.* **othlon**) *n.* paved way. Ety/370

othol *n.* stranger. PE/17:141

†**othrad** (*N.* **ostrad**) *n.* street. Ety/383

†**othronn** (*N.* **othrond**) *n.* fortress or city in underground caves, underground stronghold. Ety/379,384, WJ/414

othui (*N.* **odothui**) *adj.num.ord.* seventh. VT/42:10,25

● **oth** (*N.* **oss**) *n.* egg

ovor (*N.* **ovr**) *adj.* abundant. Ety/396, see also **ovras**

*ovra- *v.* to abound. Ety/396

ovras *n.abst.of* **ovor** crowd, heap. Ety/396

pad- *v.* to step. PE/17:34

pâd *n.* a step (action), way, road, track. WJ/387, S/438

padra- *v.* to walk. PE/17:34, S/438, WJ/387

Ⅎ **pae** *n.* vegetable

paeth *n.* speech. PE/17:126

†**paich** (*N.* **peich**) *n.* juice, syrup. Ety/382

palan- *adv.* afar, abroad, far and wide. LotR/II:I, LotR/IV:X, RGEO/72-74

***palandir-** *v.* watch from afar. Letters/427, PE/17:25

Ⅎ **palan-hinnen** *adj.* famous 'far-known'

palath I *n.* surface. Ety/380

palath II *n.* iris (the flower). RS/432, TI/114

Ⅎ **pama-** *v.* to vomit (Q. quama-)

***pan** *adj.* all, in totality. SD/129-31

pân (*N.* **pein**) *n.* plank, fixed board (especially in floor). Ety/380

panas *n.abst.of* **pân**, floor. Ety/380

†**pand** (*N.* **pann**) *n.* courtyard. Ety/380

pann *adj.* wide. Ety/380, see also **land II**

***panna- I** *v.* to open, to enlarge. Ety/380

†**panna- II** *v.* to fill. Ety/366, see also **pathra-**

pant *adj.* full. Ety/366, SD/129-31

Ⅎ **páphen** *rel. pron.* everybody

Ⅎ **par-** *v.* to peel. PE/17:171

paran *adj.* bare, naked, smooth, shaven (often applied to hills without trees). RC/433

parch I *adj.* dry. Ety/380, VT/45:5, see also **apharch**

parch II *adj.* naked (of persons). PE/17:86

parf *pl.* **perf** *n.* book. Ety/380

parth *n.* field, enclosed grassland, sward. UT/260, PM/330, RC/349

***partha-** *v.* to arrange, compose. LR/380

path *adj.* smooth. Ety/380

Ⅎ **patha-** *v.* to smooth, iron

***pathra-** *v.* to fill. Ety/366, see also **panna- II**

pathred *n.* fullness. Ety/366

†**pathu** (*N.* **pathw**) *n.* level space, sward. Ety/380

paur *n.* fist (in reference to a tighly closed hand, as in using an implement or a craft-tool, rather than to a fist used in punching). Ety/366, S/429, PM/179,318, VT/47:8

paw *n.* sickness. Ety/366

ƚ **pe** *conj.* if

ƚ **pé** *pl.* **pui** *n.* lip

***ped-** *v.* to speak, to say. LotR/II:IV, TL/21:09

pedweg *adj.* talkative, saying a lot. PE/17:144

peg *n.* small spot, dot. Ety/382

***pel-** *v.* to fade, wane. LotR/1107

pêl *pl.* **peli** *n.* fenced field, enclosure. Ety/380

***peleth** *n.* fading, withering. LotR/D

***pelia-** *v.* to spread. Ety/380

***pelin** *n.* fading, withering. Ety/366

pelthaes *n.* pivot. Ety/380, Ety/390

***pen- I** *prep.pref.* without, lacking, -less. LotR/II:II

pen II *relative pron.* one, somebody, anybody. WJ/376

penbed *adj.* unpronounceable. PE/17:145

pend (*N.* **penn**) *n.* declivity, slope. Ety/380, RC/525

pendrath (*N.* **pendrad**) *n.* passage up or down slope, stairway. Ety/380

penedh *n.* Elf, 'speaker'. PE/17:140

peng *n.Mil.* bow (for shooting). Ety/366

pengolodh *n.* teaching sage, a doctor of lore, lore-master. PE/17:139

***penia-** *v.* to fix, to set. Ety/380

ƚ **penídh** *adj.* restless

ƚ **penind** *adj.* without inner thought, insane

penna *n. and adj.* **1**. *n.* vowel **2**. *as an adj.* lacking. VT/39:17

penna- *v.* to slant down. LotR/II:I, RGEO/72

pennas *n.abst.of* **pent**, history, historical account. Ety/366, WJ/192, WJ/206

ƚ **pennig** *n.* coin

†**penninor** (*N.* **penninar**) *n.* last day of the year. Ety/400

pent *n.* tale. Ety/366

ƚ **pephen** *rel. pron.* if anybody, whoever (Q aiquen)

per- *pref.* half, divided in middle. PE/17:102

***peredhel** *n.* half-elf. S/430, LotR/A(i)

perian *n.* Hobbit, Halfling. LotR/VI:IV, LotR/E, RGEO/75, Letters/308

periannath *n. coll. of* **perian** the Hobbits, Halflings. LotR/VI:IV, LotR/E-F, RGEO/75, Letters/308

perin *adj.* half, divided in middle. Ety/380

ᚠ **pess** *n.* feather (Q quesse)

pessa- *v.* to concern, to affect. Ety/AC

pesseg *n.* pillow. Ety/366

peth *n.* word. Ety/366, LotR/II:IV, RS/463

pethron *n.* narrator, minstrel. Ety/366

ᚠ **pholg** *n.* pig

pigen *adj.* tiny. Ety/382

†**pihen** (*N.* **pichen**) *adj.* juicy. Ety/382

● **pil** *n.* colour

ᚠ **pilin** *n.* arrow

ᚠ **pim** *n.* tail (Q pimpë, pimp)

pîn *adj.* little. RC/536

pind *n.* crest, ridge; long (low) hill with a sharp ridge against the skyline. PE/17:24

pinnath *n. coll. of* **pind**, crests, ridges, group of downs. LotR/Index, RC/525

pirin *n.* a type of flower that opens and shuts quickly with changing light. PE/17:146

plad *n.* palm, flat of the hand, hand held upwards or forwards, flat and tensed (with fingers and thumb closed or spread). VT/47:9, see also **camlann, talf I**

plada- *v.* to feel with the hand, to pass the sensitive palm over a surface. VT/47:9

pôd *n.* animal's foot. Ety/382

ᚠ **pôg** *n.* bag (Q. poko)

ᚠ **pol-** *v.* to be able to (can, could)

ᚠ **por-** *v.* to choke, drown

● **porog** *n.* chicken, fowl

post *n.* pause, halt, rest, cessation, respite. Ety/382

ᚠ **posta-** *v.* to rest

*****presta-** *v.* to affect, trouble, disturb. Ety/380

prestannen *pp. of* **presta-**, **1.** affected **2.** mutated (of a mutated vowel). Ety/380

prestanneth *n.* affection of vowels, mutation. Ety/380

ᚠ **pûg** *n.* blackberry

*puia- *v.* to spit. Ety/382
puig *adj.* clean, tidy, neat. Ety/382
ꝼ puiga- *v.* to wash, to clean

Ⅎ **ractha-** *v.* to shatter

râd *n.* path, track. Ety/383

***rada-** *v.* to make a way, find a way. Ety/383

raeda- *v.* to catch in a net. VT/42:12

raef (*N.* **raew**) *n.* net. VT/42:12

†**raeg** (*N.* **rhoeg**) *adj.* crooked, bent, wrong. Ety/383

Ⅎ **raegdan** *n.* sinner

†**raen I** (*N.* **rhaen**) *adj.* crooked. Ety/382

raen II *adj.* netted, enlaced. VT/42:11

†**raew** (*N.* **rhaew**) *n.* fathom. Ety/382

● **râf** *adj.* roaring

†**rafen** (*N.* **rhafn**) *n.* wing (horn), extended point at side, etc. Ety/382

Ⅎ **rag-** *v.* to break

Ⅎ **ragui** *adj.* breakable

Ⅎ **raida-** *v.* to smile

†**rain I** (*N.* **rhain**) *n.* border. Ety/383

rain II (*N.* **rein**) *n.* erratic wandering. VT/42:13

raitha- *v.* to strive, reach for

ram (*N.* **rham**) *n.* wall. Ety/382, S/436

rammas *n.abst.of* **ram**, (great) wall. LotR/V:I, LotR/Index

†**ranc** *pl.* **renc** (*N.* **rhanc** *pl.* **rhengy**) *n.* arm. Ety/382

randír (*N.* **rhandir**) *n. masc.* wanderer, pilgrim. Ety/383, VT/42:13

rant *n.* **1.** lode, vein **2.** course, riverbed. Ety/383, S/436

***raph** *n.* rope. UT/424

rasg *n.* wagon, wain, four wheeled cart for dragging loads usually pulled by horses or oxen. PE/17:28

rass (*N.* **rhas**) *n.* horn (especially on living animal, but also applied to mountains). Ety/383, VT/46:10, LotR/E, S/436

rath *n.* **1.** course, riverbed **2.** street (in a city). Ety/383, LotR/Index, RC/523,551

†**raud** (*N.* **rhaud**) *n.* metal. Ety/383

†**raudh** (*N.* **rhaudh**) *adj.* hollow, cavernous. Ety/384

raug (*N.* **rhaug**) *n.* a powerful, hostile and terrible creature, a demon. Ety/384, S/436, WJ/415

†**raun** (*N.* **rhaun**) **1.** *adj.* errant, **2.** *n.* month, from the name of the moon as the Wanderer. Ety/383

†raw I (*N.* **rhaw**) *n.* bank (especially of a river). Ety/382

†raw II (*N.* **rhaw**) *pl.* †roe *n.* lion. Ety/383

● rêbroch *n.* zebra ('striped horse'). PE/11:64

-red *suffix.* denotes completion of a work or design, with final details and/or finishing touches. PE/17:185

†redh- (*N.* **rhedh-**) *v.* to sow. Ety/383

†rein (*N.* **rhein**) *n.* slot, spoor, track, footprint. Ety/384

rem I *n.* mesh, net (for catching, hunter's or fisher's net). LotR/E, VT/42:29

†rem II (*N.* **rhem**) *adj.* frequent, numerous. Ety/383

*remmen *pp.adj.* woven, netted, tangled. LotR/E, LotR/II:I, RGEO/72

Remmirath *n.* the constellation Pleiades, 'the netted jewels'. PE/17:24

Ⅎ ren- *v.* to remember

†rend (*N.* **rhenn**) *adj.* circular. Ety/383, VT/46:11

†renia- (*N.* ***rhenia-***) *v.* to wander, stray. Ety/383

†rest (*N.* **rhest**) *n.* cut. Ety/384

†revia- (*N.* ***rhevia-***) *v.* **1.** to fly, sail **2.** to wander. Ety/382

rhae *adj.* easy. PE/17:172

rhaed *adj.* to complete a work or design, to add finishing touches and final details. PE/17:185, see also -red

*rhach *n.* curse. MR/373

rhanc *adj.* awry, awkward. PE/17:154

rhass *n.* precipice. Ety/363

*rhavan *n.* wild man. WJ/219

rhaw I *adj.* wild, untamed. Ety/382, VT/46:10

rhaw II *n.* flesh, body. MR/350, VT/47:12

†rhib- (*N.* **thrib-**) *v.* to scratch. Ety/387

rhîw *n.* winter (in Imladris, winter was 72 days long). LotR/D

rhonn (*N.* **rhond**) *n.* body. PE/17:183

†rhosc (*N.* **rhosg**) *adj.* brown, russet. Ety/385

†rhoss (*N.* **thross**) *n.* whisper or rustling sound. Ety/386

*rhovan *n.* wilderness. LotR/Map, VT/46:10

rhovanion *n.* the Wilderland. LotR/Map

rhudol *adj.* unwelcome. PE/17:170

rhûn *n.* east. Ety/384, S/436, LotR/E

rhúnedain *n.* Easterlings. PE/17:18

rhúnen *adj.* eastern. S/420

†rhuven *n.arch.poet.* east. Ety/384

rî (*N.* **rhî**) *n.* crown, wreath, garland. Ety/383, PM/347

†**rib-** (*N.* **rhib-**) *v.* to flow like a torrent. Ety/384

rîdh *n.* sown field, acre. Ety/383, VT/46:11

***rîf** *n.* bark. LotR/E, TC/169, TC/173

***rig-** *v.* to twine, wreathe. PM/347

ril *n.* brilliance, especially used of white radiation. PE/17:47

rim I (*N.* **rhim**) *n.* crowd, host, great number. Ety/383, S/436, Letters/178,382

†**rim II** (*N.* **rhim**) *n.* cold pool or lake (in mountains). Ety/384

†**rîn I** (*N.* **rhîn**) *n. and adj.* **1.** crowned **2.** *as a noun, by ext.* crowned lady, queen. Ety/393, Ety/389

rîn II *n.* remembrance. PM/372

ꝼ **rínas** *n.abst.of* **rîn II** memory

†**rinc** (*N.* **rhinc**) *n.* twitch, jerk, trick, sudden move. Ety/383

†**rind** (*N.* **rhind, rhinn**) *n.* circle. Ety/383

ring (*N.* **rhing**) *adj.* cold. Ety/383, S/436, VT/42:13

†**ringorn** (*N.* **rhingorn**) *n.* circle. Ety/365

†**rîs** (*N.* **rhîs**) *n. fem.* queen. Ety/383, see also **bereth**

†**riss** (*N.* **rhiss**) *n. and adj.* **1.** ravine, cleft **2.** cloven, separate. Ety/384

†**rista-** (*N.* ***rhista-**) *v.* **1.** to cut **2.** to rend, rip. Ety/384

†**ritha-** (*N.* ***rhitha-**) *v.* to jerk, twitch, snatch. Ety/383

†**rîw** (*N.* **rhîf**) *n.* brink, brim, edge, hem, border. Ety/383

roch *n.* horse, swift horse for riding. Ety/384, S/436, Letters/178,282,382

rochben *n.* (horse) rider. WJ/376

rochir *n.* horse-lord, knight (in Gondorian Sindarin this was spelt and pronounced as **rohir**). Letters/178, LotR, see also **rochirrim**

rochirrim (*N.* **rohiroth**) *n. class pl. of* **rochir**, horse lords, the people of Rohan (in Gondorian Sindarin this was spelt and pronounced as **rohirrim**). Letters/178, LotR, UT/318

rochon *n.* (horse) rider. UT/463

***rodon** *n.* Ainu, divinity, 'noble one'. LotR/D

ꝼ **rogol** *n.* saddle

ꝼ **rohaith** *n.Mil.* lancer 'horse-spear'

rom (*N.* **rhom**) *n.* horn, trumpet. WJ/400

†**romru** (*N.* **rhomru**) *n.* sound of horns. Ety/384

rond (*N.* **rhonn**) *n.* **1.** cave roof **2.** vaulted or arched roof, as seen from below (and usually not visible from outside), or a (large) hall of chamber so roofed. Ety/384, VT/46:12, S/437, WJ/414

†**ross I** (*N.* **rhoss**) *n.* rain. Ety/384

ross II *adj.* red-haired, copper coloured (especially used of animals, as fox, red deer, etc.). VT/41:10

Ⅎ **rosseg** *n.* raindrop

rost *adj.* rainy. S/220

*****rosta-** *v.* to hollow out, excavate. Ety/384

*****roval** *n.* pinion, great wing (of eagle). LotR/VI:IV, Ety/382

†**rû** (*N.* **rhû**) *n.arch.poet.* loud-sound, trumpet-sound. Ety/384

rûdh *adj.* bald. S/379, WJ/187

†**rui** (*N.* **rhui**) *n.* hunt, hunting. Ety/384

ruin *adj.* (fiery) red. PM/366

ruist *n.* fireplace, hearth. PE/17:183

Ⅎ **run-** *v.* to polish, grind, rub. PE/17:89

rusc *n.* fox. VT/41:10

rust *n.* copper. VT/41:10

rustui *adj.* of copper. VT/41:10

rûth *n.* anger. S/436

● **ruthol** *n.* oats, porridge. PE/11:86

ruthra- *v.* to rage. PE/17:188

Ⅎ **rúthui** *adj.* angry

†**rŷn** (*N.* **rhŷn**) *n.* 'chaser', hound of chase. Ety/384

ꝼ **saba-** *v.* to delve

***sabar** *n.* delved mine. WJ/209,419, S/380, PE/12:82

sad *n.* limited area naturally or artificially defined, a place, spot. UT/425, VT/42:19-20

sâdh *n.* sward, turf. VT/42:20

sador *adj.* trusty, steadfast, loyal. PE/17:183

sadron *n.masc.* faithful one, loyal companion. UT/431

sael *adj.* wise. MR/305, SD/129-31, WJ/233

ꝼ **saelas** *n.abst.of* **sael** wisdom

saer *adj.* bitter. Ety/385

saew *n.* poison. Ety/385

saf- *v.* to have, to possess. PE/17:173, see also **gar-**

said *adj.* private, separate, not common, excluded. VT/42:20

● **saig** *adj.* hungry. PE/11:66

†**sain** (*N.* **sein**) *adj.* new. Ety/385, see also **cîw, eden, gwain**

salab *n.* herb. Ety/385

ꝼ **salf** *n.* lyre (Q salma)

● **salfin** *n.* viola

● **salfinnel** *n.* violin

†**salph** (*N.* **salff**) *n.* broth, liquid food, soup. Ety/385, VT/45:12

***sam** *n.* chamber, room. LotR/VI:III, S/435, see also **sammath**

ꝼ **sam-** *v.* to think

samarad *n. dual pl. of* **sammar**, two neighbours. VT/48:20

sammar *n.* neighbor, 'one who dwells beside'. VT/48:20

sammath *n. coll. of* **sam**, chambers. LotR/VI:III, S/435

sant *n.* garden, field, yard (or other place in private ownership whether enclosed or not). VT/42:20

sarch *n.* grave. UT/463

ꝼ **sarf** *n.* table

sarn *n.* **1.** stone (as a material) **2.** small stone, pebble. Ety/385, RC/327, S/437, UT/463, VT/42:11

sarnas *n.abst.of* **sarn**, cairn, pile of stones. LR/406

saur *adj.* bad, putrid (of food). PE/17:183

sautha- *v.* to drain. Ety/388

saw I *pl.* †**soe** (*N. pl.* **sui**) *n.* juice. Ety/385

saw II *n.* filth, putrescence. PE/17:183

seidia- *v.* to set aside, appropriate to a special purpose or owner. VT/42:20

sell *n. fem.* **1.** daughter **2.** girl, maid (child). Ety/385

sellath *n. coll. of* **sell**, all the daughters. SD/129-31

*****sen** *adj. dem.* this. LotR/II:IV

*****senn** (*N.* **send**) *n.* rest. RC/523

sennas *n. abst. of* **senn**, guesthouse, resting place. RC/523

sennui *adv.* rather, instead. SD/129-31

sera- *v.* to like. LotR

sereg *n.* blood. PE/17:184, see also **agar**, **iâr**

seregon *n.* 'Blood of Stone', a plant known in English as 'stonecrop', with deep red flowers that grew on Amon Rûdh. S/437

seron *n.* lover. PM/348

serni *n.* pebble bank, shingle, also the name of a river in Gondor. VT/42:10

sí *adv.* here. PE/17:27,67

● **sibtha-** *v.* to whistle

sîdh *n.* peace. Ety/385

sigil I *n.Mil.* dagger, knife. Ety/385

sigil II *n.* necklace. WJ/258

síla- *v.* to shine white. LB/354

silevril *n.* Silmaril. Ety/373, see also **golovir**, **mirion**

silivren *adj.* (white) glittering. LotR/II:I, RGEO/72

Ⱦ **sim** *n.* pipe, flute (Q simpa)

Ⱦ **sing** *n.* salt

Ⱦ **singren** *adj.* salty

siniath *n. coll.* news, tidings. Ety/385

sinnarn *n.* novel tale. Ety/385

sír *adv.* today. VT/44:21,27

sîr *n.* river. Ety/385, S/437, RC/384, see also **sirion**

*****siria-** *v.* to flow. Ety/385

sirion *n. augm. of* **sîr**, great river. Ety/385

sirith *n.* flowing. VT/42:11

*****soga-** *v.* to drink. Ety/388, VT/46:16

solch *n.* root (especially as edible). Ety/388

Ⱦ **soth** *n.* bath

sui *conj.* as, like. VT/44:27

*__suil__ *n.* greeting. LotR/A(ii), see also __suilad__

*__suila-__ *v.* to greet. SD/129-31

__suilad__ *ger. of* __suila-__, greeting. SD/129

*__suilanna-__ *v.* to greet, to give greetings. SD/129-31

†__suith__ (N. __sûth__) *n.* draught (of a drink). Ety/388

ⅎ __suithlas__ *n.* tea 'leaf draught'

__sûl I__ *n.* wind (that can be heard, not seen). S/437

__sûl II__ *n.* goblet. Ety/388

● __sus__ *interj.* shush!

tachol (*N.* **tachl**) *n.* pin, brooch, clasp. PE/18:100

tâd (*N.* **tad**) *adj. num. card.* two. Ety/349, Ety/391, WJ/388, VT/42:25-27, VT/48:6

***tad-dal** *pl.* **tad-dail** *n. and adj.* biped, two-legged animal. WJ/388

tadol *adj. num. quant.* double. Ety/391

tadui *adj. num. ord.* second. VT/42:25

taeg *n.* boundary, limit, boundary line. WJ/309

taen I *n.* height, summit of high mountain. Ety/389

taen II *adj.* long (and thin). Ety/391

taer I *adj.* straight. Ety/392, VT/46:18

taer II *adj.* lofty, tall, high. PE/17:186

taes *n.* nail. Ety/390

***taetha-** *v.* to fasten, tie. Ety/389

taew *n.* holder, socket, hasp, clasp, staple. Ety/390, VT/46:17

Ɍ **taf-** *v.* to taste

tafen (*N.* **tavn**) *n.* a thing made by handicraft. PE/17:107

***tagol** *n.* post, mark. VT/42:8,28

taid *adj.* second (in the sense of supporting, second in command). VT/42:25

†**taith** (*N.* **teith**) *n.* mark. Ety/391

tâl (*N.* **teil**) *n.* foot. UT/313

talad *n.* an incline, slope. Ety/390

talaf *n.* ground, floor. Ety/390

†**talagan** (*N.* **talagand**) *n.* harper. Ety/377

talan *n.* flet, wooden platform (in the trees of Lothlórien where the Galadhrim dwelt). UT/465, LotR/II:VI

talath (*N.* **dalath**) *n.* **1.** flat surface, plane **2.** flat land, plain, (wide) valley. UT/465, Ety/353, S/437

†**talf I** (*N.* **dalf**) *n.* palm of hand. Ety/353, see also **camlann, plad**

talf II *n.* flat field, flat land, wang. PE/17:52

***talif** *n.* ankle 'foot link'. PE/11:42,69

***talraph** *n.* stirrup, 'foot rope'. UT/424

talt *adj.* slipping, falling, insecure. Ety/390

†**talu** (*N.* **dalw**) *adj.* flat. Ety/353

***tamma-** *v.* to knock. Ety/390

tân *n.* builder, smith, wright, artificer. PE/17:27

tanc *adj.* firm. Ety/389

tang *n.Mil.* bowstring. Ety/394

*****tangada-** *v.* to make firm, confirm, establish. Ety/389

tann *n.* sign. MR/385

tanngyl (*N.* **taengyl**) *n.* Venus 'the signifier'. MR/385

tara (*N.* **tar-**) *adj.* tough, stiff. Ety/390

tarag *n.* **1.** horn **2.** *by ext.,* steep mountain peak. Ety/391, VT/46:17

tarch *adj.* stiff, tough. RC/536

tarias *n. abst.* stiffness, toughness, difficulty. Ety/390

tarlanc *adj.* proud, obstinate, 'stiff-necked'. PE/17:092, RC/536

Ⅎ **tarlangas** *n.* pride

Ⅎ **tartha-** *v.* to crucify (TARA-)

Ⅎ **taru** *n.* cross, crucifix (Q **tarwë**)

tass (*N.* **tars**) *n.* labour, task. Ety/391

tathar (*N.* **tathor**) *n.* willow-tree. PE/17:81

tathren *adj.* of willow, having willows. SA

taug *adj.* strong, firm. PE/17:115

taur I *n.* king (only used of the legitimate kings of whole tribes). Ety/389, Ety/395, see also **aran**

taur II *n.* great wood, forest. LotR/469,1134, PE/17:82,115

taur III *adj.* mighty, vast, overwhelming, huge, awful, high, sublime. Ety/391

Ⅎ **tauras** *n.abst.of* **taur III** vastness

tauron *n.* forester. PM/358

taus *n.* thatch. Ety/395

tavor (*N.* **tavr**) *n.* woodpecker (bird), 'knocker'. Ety/390

taw *adj.* of wool, woollen. Ety/394

tawar *n.* **1.** wood (as a material) **2.** *by ext.,* great wood, forest. UT/467, Ety/391

tawaren *adj.* wooden. Ety/391

tawarwaith *n. class pl. of* **tawar**, Silvan elves, 'forest elves'. UT/256

tê *n.* line, way. Ety/391

tegil (*N.* **tegol**) *n.* pen. PM/318 Ety/391

tegilbor *n.* one skilled in calligraphy, a calligrapher. PM/318

*****teitha-** *v.* to write, draw. Ety/391, LotR/II:IV

telch *n.* **1.** leg **2.** stem. Ety/391

tele *pl.* **telei** *N. n.* end, rear, hindmost part. Ety/392

teler *n.* an Elf, one of the Teleri. PM/385

telerrim *n.class pl. of* **teler**, the Teleri, a tribe of Elves. PM/385

*telia- (*N.* *teilia-) *v.* to play. Ety/395

telien (*N.* teilien) *n.* sport, play. Ety/395

ꟻ tell *n.* **1.** a grade **2.** a step in a stairway or ladder

tellen (*N.* tellein) *n.* sole of foot. Ety/384

ꟻ teltha- *v.* to finish, end, cease

telu *n.* dome, high roof. Ety/391

*ten *object pron.* him/her/it. VT/44:21,25-6

ꟻ tengia- *v.* to reveal

ꟻ tengwa- *v.* to read (written material), see also **henna-**

tess *n.* (fine pierced) hole. Ety/AC

têw *pl.* tîw *n.* letter, written sign. Ety/391, WJ/396, LotR/II:IV, LotR/E, Letters/427

ꟻ téwgiled *n.* spelling (Q tengwacilme, PE/22)

tha, thá *adv.* then, next. PE/22:97

thafen (*N.* thafn) *n.* post, wooden pillar. Ety/387

thala *adj.* stalwart, steady, firm. Ety/388

thalion *pl.* thelyn *n.* hero, dauntless man. Ety/388, S/438

tham (*N.* thamb) *n.* hall. Ety/387, see also **thamas**

thamas (*N.* thambas) *n. abst. of* **tham**, great hall. Ety/387

thanc *adj.* cleft, split, forked. S/415, Ety/388

*thand I *n.Mil.* shield. UT/281-282

thand II (*N.* thann) *adj.* firm, true, abiding. Ety/388

thang *n.* compulsion, duress, need, oppression. PE/17:116

thangail *n.Mil.* shield-fence, a battle formation of the Dúnedain. UT/281-282

thangorodrim *n.* 'mountains of oppression' or 'mountains of tyranny', the mountains that surrounded the stronghold of Morgoth. MR/298, PE/17:116

ꟻ thann *n.* law, commandment, rule (cf. Q. sanyë)

ꟻ thannas *n.abst.of* **thand II** truth

thâr *n.* stiff, dry grass. Ety/388

thar- *pref.* across, athwart, over, beyond. Ety/388, S/438

tharan *adj.* vigorous. PE/17:27

tharas *n.* hassock, footstool. Ety/388

tharbad *n.* cross-way. S/438

tharn *adj.* sapless, stiff, rigid, withered. Ety/388

thaur *adj.* abominable, abhorrent. S/438

thavron *n.* carpenter, wright, builder. Ety/388

thaw *adj.* corrupt, rotten. Ety/393

thel- *v.* to intend, mean, purpose, resolve, will. WJ/318-319

thela *n.* point (of spear). Ety/388

*****thelion** *n.* one who remains firm in his purpose. WJ/318

thenn (*N.* **thent**) *adj.* short. VT/42:29, Ety/388, UT/146, WJ/311,315, see also estent

thî *adv.* now. PE/17:27

*****thia-** *v.* to appear, seem. Ety/392

*****thilia-** *v.* to glisten. Ety/392, VT/46:18

thîn *n.poet.* evening. Ety/392, VT/46:18

Thindrim *n.class.pl.* Sindar Elves, 'grey elves'. VT/41:9

thinn (*N.* **thind**) *adj.* grey, pale. Ety/392, S/438

thinna- *v.* to fade, to grow towards evening. Ety/392

thinnas *n.abst.of* **thent**, 'shortness' (name of a mark indicating short quality of vowel). Ety/388

Thinnedhel *n.* Sinda, a subject of Thingol, 'Grey Elf'. PE/17:139

thîr *n.* look, face, expression, countenance. Ety/392, VT/41:10

thôl *n.Mil.* helm. S/438

thôn (*N.* **thaun**) *n.* pine-tree. Ety/392, S/438, RC/384

thond *n.* root (of a tree, plant etc.). LotR/E, Letters/178

*****thoniel** *n. fem.* kindler. PE/17:82

thôr *adj.* swooping, leaping down. Ety/393

*****thora-** *v.* to fence. Ety/393

thórod *n.* torrent. Ety/393

thoron *n.* eagle. Ety/392, S/438

thoronath *n. coll. of* **thoron**, eagles. S/387,438

thoronhîn *n.* Eorlingas, the muster of the Rohirrim. PE/22:159

thost *n.* smell. VT/46:19

*****thosta-** *v.* to stink. VT/46:19

thû *n.* stench. Ety/393

*****thuia-** *v.* to breathe. Ety/393

ꝼ **thuith** *n.* resin, sap

thûl *n.* breath. Ety/393

thurin *adj.* secret, hidden. LB/304, Ety/394

tî *n.* line, row. Ety/392

till (*N.* **tild**) *n.* horn, point. Ety/393

tin *n.* spark, sparkle, especially used of stars. PE/17:39

*tîn *adj. poss. 3rd* his/hers/its. SD/129-31

tinc *n.* metal. Ety/394

*tinna- *v.* to glint. Ety/393

tinnu (*N.* **tindu**) *n.* **1.** dusk, twilight, early night (without Moon) **2.** *by ext.* starry twilight. Ety/355, Ety/393

ᚠ **Tinnulín** *n.* Arcturus, 'the glint at dusk', the brightest star in the northern celestial hemisphere

tint *n.* spark, small star. Ety/393

tîr *adj.* straight, right. Ety/391

*tir- *v.* to look towards, watch over, guard. Ety/394

*tíra- *v.* to see. SD/129-31

ᚠ **tíras** *n.abst.of* **tîr** straightness, correctness

tiria- *v.* to watch, gaze, ward, guard. Ety/394, PE/17:25

tirith *n.* watch, guard, vigilance. Ety/394, S/437, Letters/158, VT/42:11

*tirnen *pp. of* **tir-**, guarded. UT/465, Ety/394, S/437

tithen *adj.* little, tiny. Ety/394

tiwdi *n.* alphabet. Ety/AC

*toba- *v.* to cover, roof over. Ety/394

tobas *n.abst.of* **toba-**, roofing, roof. Ety/394

tofen (*N.* **tofn**) *adj.* low-lying, deep, low. Ety/394

*tog- *v.* to lead, bring. Ety/395

● **togol** *n.* cockerel

tol *n.* island, (steep) isle rising with sheer sides from the sea or from a river. RC/333, VT/47:28

tol- *v.* to come, approach (in both space and time). Ety/395, PE/22:168

toleg (*N.* **tolch**) *n. dim.* **1.** 'little prominent one', play name given to the middle finger (Elvish play-name used by and taught to children). VT/48:6,16-17

tolog *adj.* stalwart, trusty. Ety/395

toloth (*N.* **tolodh**) *adj. num. card.* eight. Ety/394, VT/42:25, VT/42:31, VT/48:6

tolothen *adj. num. ord.* eighth. This may be just Gondorian Sindarin. SD/129, see also **tolthui**

ᚠ **tolothil** *n.* octagon 'eight points'

*toltha- *v.* to fetch, summon, make come. Ety/395

tolthui (*N.* **tollui**) *adj. num. ord.* eighth. VT/42:10,25,27

tond (*N.* **tonn**) *adj.* tall. Ety/395

tong *adj.* taut, tight (of strings), resonant. Ety/394

ᚠ tor- *v.* to hide

tôr *n.masc.arch.* brother. Ety/394, the word **muindor** is more usual

torech *n.* (secret) hole, excavation, lair. PE/17:89,188, RC/491

torn *n.* down, burial mound. PE/17:116, see also **haudh**

torog *n.* troll. LotR/1132, PE/17:136

*tortha- *v.* to wield, control. Ety/395

toss *n.* bush, low-growing tree (as maple, hawthorn, blackthorn, holly, etc.). Ety/379,395

*trann *n.* shire, administrative district, division of a realm. SD/129-31

*trannail *adj.* of the Shire. SD/129-31

trasta- *v.* to harass, trouble. Ety/391

tre- (*N.* **tri**) *pref.* through (denoting completeness when prefixed to verbs). Ety/392

*trenar- *v.* to recount, to tell to end. Ety/374

trenarn *n.* account, tale. Ety/374

*trevad- *v.* to traverse. Ety/352

trî *prep.* through. Ety/392

trîw *adj.* fine, slender. Ety/392

tû *n.* muscle, sinew, vigour, physical strength. Ety/394

tûg *adj.* thick, fat. Ety/394

*tuia- *v.* **1.** to sprout, spring **2.** to swell. Ety/394

ᚠ tûd *n.* thigh

tui *n.* a sprout, bud. Ety/369

tuilinn *n.* swallow, bird 'spring-singer'. Ety/369

ᚠ tulf *n.* bier, frame on which a coffin is carried to a grave (Q. tulma)

ᚠ tull *n.* banner, standard

tulu *n.* support, prop. Ety/395

tulus *n.* poplar-tree. Ety/395

tum *n.* deep valley, under or among hills. SA

tump *n.* hump. Ety/395

tund (*N.* **tunn**) *n.* hill, mound. Ety/395

tûr *n.* **1.** master **2.** mastery, victory. SA

● túrcham *n.* throne 'victory-chair' (GL)

● tûs- *v.* to tease, comb wool

ú- *pref. interj. and adv.* no, not. LotR/1061, PE/17:62,144, UT/313, VT/42:33, VT/44:28, WJ/369

úan *n.* monster. Ety/351

uanui *adj.* monstrous, hideous. Ety/351

ubed *n.* denial. WR/137

úbedui *adj.* not fit to say, unspeakable. PE/17:144

ⅎ **úchannas** *n.* unintelligence

Udûn *n.* Hell, dark pit. The name of Morgoth's first underground stronghold, and a plain in Mordor. SD/34

úgal *adj.* dark, not shining. PE/17:144

úgar *adj.* idle. PE/17:144

úgarol *adj.* idling. PE/17:144

*****úgarth** *pl.* **úgerth** *n.* bad deed, sin, trespass. VT/44:21,28

ui I *n.* envelope (especially of the Outer Sea or Air enfolding the world within the Ilurambar or world-walls). Ety/397

ui, ui- **II** *adv. and pref.* ever. Ety/357, Letters/278

uial *n.* twilight. Ety/400, S/439, LotR/D

*****uidafnen** *adj.* ever-closed. WR/341

uil *n.* seaweed. Ety/396, see also **gaeruil**

uilos *n.and adj.* **1.** always white, ever white as snow **2.** *as a noun,* a small white everlasting flower also called simbelmynë or 'evermind'. RGEO/74, Letters/278, UT/55

uin *prep.* of the. SD/129-31

uir *n.* eternity. Ety/379

uireb *adj.* eternal. Ety/379

● **uitha-** *v.* to lay eggs, nest

ul- *pref.* ugly. Ety/378

ûl *n.* odour. Ety/378

ⅎ **úlaer** *n.* Nazgûl, 'unholy'. (Q. úlairi)

úlal *adj.* grave, serious. PE/17:144

ulu *n.* one of the names of the Vala Ulmo. Ety/396

uluithiad *adj.* unquenchable, without quenching. SD/62

● **ulum** *n.* camel

†**ulunn** (*N.* **ulun**) *n.* monster, deformed and hideous creature. Ety/396

um *adj.* bad, evil. Ety/396

ûn *n.* creature. Ety/379

ungol *n.* spider. Ety/366, WR/202, LotR, RC/490

ûr I *n.* fire, heat. Ety/396

ûr II *adj.* wide. Ety/396, see also **land II**

ⴕ **úragui** *adj.* unbreakable

urug *n.* **1.** Orc (rarely used) **2.** *arch.* 'bogey'; anything that caused fear to the Elves, any dubious shape, shadow or prowling creature. WJ/390, see also **orch, glam**

urui *n. and adj.* **1.** hot **2.** *as a noun,* the month of August. LotR/1110

úthaes *n.* inducement to do wrong, temptation. VT/44:30

ⴕ **úthannas** *n.* untruth

úvel *adj.* not loving, unloving. PE/17:145

úvelui *adj.* unlovable. PE/17:145

ylf *n.* drinking-vessel. WJ/416

ŷr (*N.* **iôr**) *n.* course. Ety/400

Yssion (*N.* **Gaerys**) *n.* a name for the Maia Ossë. WJ/400

English - Sindarin

A

abandon *v.* awartha-
abandonment *n.* awarth
abhor *v.* fuia-
abhorrence *n.* delos
abhorrent *adj.* thaur
abiding *adj.* him I, thand II
abominable *adj.* deleb, thaur
abound *v.* ovra-
about *prep.* o II
above I *prep.* or
above II *pref.* or-
abundant *adj.* ovor
abyss *n.* dath, iâ
accommodate *v.* camtha-
account *n.* trenarn
account (of tongues) *n.* lammas
acorn *n.* breth
acre *n.* rîdh
across *adv. pref.* ath- I, athra- I, thar-
active *adj.* carweg, legol
acute *adj.* laeg I
adhere *v.* himia-
afar *adv.pref.* palan-
affect *v.* pessa-, presta-
affected *pp.* prestannen
affection *n.* mîl
affliction *n.* caul
after *prep.* ab
after (when discussing time) *prep.* cad
aged *n.* iphant
agile *adj.* celeg
ago *adv.* io
after *prep.pref* ab-
again *adv.* adui
against *prep.* dan
ah! *interj.* ai!
Ainu *n.* rodon
air (as a tune) *n.* lind
air (as substance) *n.* gwelu
air (as a region) *n.* gwilith
air, lower *n.* gwelwen
alas *interj.* nae

Aldebaran *n.* borgil
alive I *adj.* cuin
alive II *v.* cuina-
all *adj.* pân II
allegiance, hold *v.* buia-
allow *v.* daf-
alone I *pref.* er-
alone II *adj.* erui
alone III *adv.* ero
alphabet *n.* tiwdi
alphabet, runic *n.* angerthas, certhas
also *adv.* eithro
amber *n.* maligon
ambidextrous *n.* adforgam
amputate *v.* osgar-
anchor *n.* círam
ancient *adj.* iaur
and *conj.* a, ah, ar, adh
anger *n.* oroth, rûth
angle *n.* bennas, nass
angry *adj.* rúthui
angular *adj.* negen
animal *n.* celf, lavan
ankle *n.* talif
annals *n.* ínias
anniversary *n.* edinor
answer I *n.* dangweth
answer II *v.* aphed-
anvil *n.* onin
apparition, vague *n.* auth II
appear *v.* thia-
apple *n.* orf
apple-tree *n.* orforn
approach *v.* anglenna-
April *n.* gwirith
arch *n.* cû
Arcturus *n.* tinnulín
arid *adj.* apharch
arm *n.* ranc
around *pref.* os-
arrange *v.* partha-
arrow *n.* pilin
article *n.* bach

artificer *n.* tân

as *conj.* sui

ash *n.* lith

ashen *adj.* lithui

ask *v.* mabed-

assemble *v.* cova-

assembly *n.* hûd

assist *v.* natha-

at *prep.* na

August *n.* urui

Aulë *n.* belegol

author *n.* narnvaeron

autumn *n.* iavas, lasbelin

autumn (late) *n.* firith

Avar *n.* gavar, morben, morbenedh

avarice *n.* arasaith

avenge *v.* achar-

awaken *v.* echuia-

awakening *n.* echui

awe *n.* anwar

awful *adj.* gaer I

awkward *adj.* rhanc

awry *adj.* rhanc

axe-stroke *n.* hast

B

babble *v.* glavra-

babbling *adj.* glavrol

baby *n.* laes

back, again *adv. pref.* ad-

back, from shoulder to shoulder *n.* bost

bad *adj.* faeg, um

bag *n.* pôg

bake *v.* basta-

bald *adj.* rûdh

ball *n.* coron

ban *v.* boda-

bane *n.* dagnir

banner *n.* tull

bare *adj.* paran

bark *n.* rîf

barrow *n.* gorthad

bat *n.* blabor

bath *n.* soth

battle I *n.* auth, dagor, maeth

battle II *v.* dagra-

battles, all of the *n.* dagorath

bay *n.* côf

bay, small and land-locked *n.* hûb

be *v.* na-

be able to *v.* pol-

beach *n.* falas

beacon *n.* narthan

bear I *n.* brôg, graw, medli

bear II *v.* col-

bear-like *adj.* medlin

beard *n.* fang

bearer *n.* cyll

beat *v.* dringa-

beautiful *adj.* bain

beauty *n.* bainas

become *v.* ola-

bed *n.* haust

bedridden *adj.* caeleb

bee *n.* nui

bee, honey *n.* glinui

beech-tree *n.* brethil, fêr

before (in space) *prep.* ob

before (in time) *prep.* eb

beget *v.* edonna-, onna-

begin (suddenly and vigorously) *v.* heria-

be gone! *interj.* ego

behind *prep.* adel

behold! *interj.* alae

beneath I *pref.* di-

beneath II *prep.* nu

bent *adj.* cûn, raeg

beside *pref.* ar- (arch.)

betray *v.* gweria-

betrayer *n.* gwarth

between *prep.* im III

beyond *prep.* Athan

big *adj.* beleg

bier *n.* tulf

bind *v.* gwedh-, nod-

biped *n.* tad-dal

birch *n.* hwinn

bird, small *n.* aew, fileg

birds, of *adj.* aewen

birthday *n.* oronnad

bite *v.* nag-

biting *n.* naeth, narch

bitter *adj.* saer

black *adj.* morn

blackberry *n.* pûg

blade, axe or broadsword *n.* hathol

blasphemy *n.* daebeth

bleat *v.* neta-

bless *v.* aina-, alia-

blessing *n.* galu

blind *adj.* dom

blood *n.* agar, iâr, sereg

bloodstained *adj.* agarwaen

blossom *v.* edlothia-

blue *adj.* luin

blue, pale *adj.* elu

boar *n.* caragpholg

boat *n.* lunt

body *n.* rhaw II, rhonn

bogey *n.* urug

bold *adj.* beren, cand

bond *n.* gwedh, gwend I
bone *n.* asg
book *n.* parf
border *n.* edrain, glân II, rain I, rîw
born *pp.* onnen
born (later) *n. and adj.* abonnen
bosom *n.* ammos
bottle *n.* olph
bound *adj.* naud
bound (to limit) *v.* gleina-
boundary *n.* taeg
boundary, mark of *n.* glandagol
bow I *v.* caf-
bow II *n.Mil.* cû, peng
bowed *adj.* cûn
bowstring *n.* tang
box *n.* colch
bracelet *n.* mírechor
branch *n.* golf
brand *n.* iolf
bread *n.* bass
bread-giver *n.* bassoneth
break *v.* rag-
breakable *adj.* ragui
break out, suddenly *v.* breitha-
breast *n.* ammos
breastplate *n.* ammas
breath *n.* hwest, thûl
breathe *v.* thuia-
breeze *n.* hwá, hwest
bride *n.* dineth, dîs
bridegroom *n.* daer II
bridge *n.* iant
bright *adj.* glân I
brilliance *n.* aglar, ril
brilliance, gleaming (of the sun) *n.* fael II
brilliant *adj.* celair
brim *n.* rîw
bring *v.* tog-
bring (together) *v.* covad-
brink *n.* rîw
broad *adj.* land II
brooch *n.* tachol

broth *n.* salph
brother *n.* hanar, tôr (arch.)
brother, dear *n.* muindor
brother, sworn *n.* gwador
brown *adj.* rhosc
brown, golden/yellow/dark *adj.* baran
bud *n.* tui
builder *n.* tân
building *n.* adab, car
building, large of masonry (used as a dwelling) *n.* barthan
bull *n.* mund
burden, great *n.* caul
burial mound *n.* haudh, torn
burn *v.* dosta-
bush *n.* toss
busy *adj.* carweg
but *prep.* ach
butter *n.* mang
butterfly *n.* gwilwileth
buttocks *n.* hach

cage *n.* gadoras
cairn *n.* sarnas
cake *n.* cram
calendar *n.* genediad
call I *v.* can-, ialla-
call II *n.* ial
calligrapher *n.* tegilbor
camel *n.* ulum
camp *n.* echad
candle *n.* ligum
canopy *n.* daedelu, orthelian
cape (headland) *n.* cast
captain *n.* hest
carpenter *n.* thavron
carpet *n.* farf
carry *v.* col-
Cassiopeia *n.* gwilwileth
cat *n.* iaul
cat, queen *n.* miaulin
cat, tom *n.* miaug
catch *v.* gad-
catch (in a net) *v.* raeda-
cave *n.* fela, gathrod, groth
cavern *n.* gath
cavernous *adj.* raudh
centre *n.* ened
chain *n.* angwedh
chair *n.* ham
chamber *n.* sam
chambers *n.pl.* sammath
chance *v.* amartha-
change *v.* eichia-
character (of a story) *n.* narphen
charm *n.* lûth
cheat *v.* gweria-
cheese *n.* cur
cherry *n.* aep
cherry tree *n.* aeborn
chicken *n.* porog
child *n.* hên
choke *v.* por-
choose *v.* caw-, cil-

circle *n.* rind, ringorn
circle, outer *n.* echor
circular *adj.* rend
citadel *n.* ost
city, above ground *n.* caras
city, underground *n.* othronn
city, with a citadel or wall *n.* minas, ost
clamour *n.* caun I
clasp *n.* tachol, taew
claw *n.* gamp
clean I *adj.* puig
clean II *v.* puiga-
clear *adj.* lim II
cleared *adj.* laden
clearing (in forest) *n.* lant I
cleaver *n.Mil.* crist, hâdh
cleft I *n.* cîl I, cirith, iau II, riss
cleft II *adj.* thanc
cleft, deep *n.* falch
clever *adj.* maen
cliff *n.* îf
cliff, great *n.* brass II
cloak I *n.* coll III
cloak II *v.* fanna-
close *v.* hol-
closed *adj.* hollen
cloth *n.* lann
clothe *v.* hab-, hamma-
clothing *n.* hammad
cloud *n.* fain, fân, faun
cloudy *adj.* fanui
cloven *adj.* riss
club *n.Mil.* grond
coat, fur *n.* heleth
cobweb *n.* lhing
cockerel *n.* togol
coin *n.* pennig
coin, used in Gondor *n.* mirian
cold *adj.* ring
cold, bitter *n.* helch
colour *n.* pil
come *v.* tol-
commanding *adj.* conui

commandment *n.* thann
commonly *adj.* órui
complain *v.* muia-
complete (a work or design) *adj.* rhaed
compose *v.* partha-
composer *n.* glirvaeron
compulsion *n.* thang
conceal *v.* delia-, doltha-
conceive (an idea) *v.* nautha-
concern *v.* pessa-
confirm *v.* tangada-
conquer *v.* orthor-
consonant *n.* lamdaen
continually *adv.* him I
contorted *adj.* norn
contract *n.* gowest
control *v.* tortha-
converse *n.* athrabeth
cool *adj.* him II
copper *n.* raud, rust
copper, of *adj.* rustui
copper-coloured *adj.* gaer II, ross II
cord *n.* nordh
core *n.* ened
corn *n.* iau I
corner *n.* bennas, nass
corpse *n.* daen
correctness *n.* tíras
corrupt *adj.* thaw
counsel *v.* gor-
count *v.* gonod-, nedia-
countenance *n.* thîr
countless *adj.* arnediad, aronoded
course *n.* ŷr
courtyard *n.* pand
cover *v.* toba-
cow, milk *n.* gach
craft *n.* curu, maenas
creature *n.* ûn
creature, living *n.* gwê
crescent *n.* cû
crest *n.* pind
crime *n.* oew

crook (shape) *n.* gamp
crooked *adj.* raeg, raen I
cross I *n.* taru
cross II *v.* athra- II, athrada-
cross, to and fro *v.* athra- II
crossing *n.* athrad, iach
cross-way *n.* tharbad
crow *n.* corch
crowd *n.* hoth, ovras, rim I
crown *n.* rî
crowned *adj.* rîn I
crucifix *n.* taru
crucify *v.* tartha-
cruel *adj.* balch, baug
cruelty *n.* balchas
cry *n.* ial
cry (of encouragement in battle) *n.* hûl
cry (out) *v.* can-, nalla-
crystal *n.* ivor
crystalline *adj.* ivren
cucumber *n.* colost
Cuiviénien *n.* nen echui
cunning *adj.* coru
curse *n.* rhach
cushion *n.* nedhu
custody *n.* band
custom *n.* haew
cut I *n.* criss, rest
cut II *v.* rista-
cutlass *n.* lang
cycle, age *n.* andrann

daddy *n.* ada
daffodil *n.* maloglin
dagger *n.* sigil I
daily *adj.* ilaurui, órui
daisy *n.* eirien
damp *adj.* nîd
dance I *n.* lilth
dance II *v.* liltha-
dangle *v.* glinga-
dare *v.* bertha-
dark I *adj.* doll, dûr, morn
dark II *n.* môr
dark III (not shining) *adj.* úgal
darkness *n.* dúath, fuin, môr
daughter *n.* iell, sell
day *n.* arad, aur, calan
day, fifth of the week *n.* ormenel
day, first of the week *n.* orgilion
day, first of the year *n.* mininor
day, fourth of the week *n.* orgaladh, orgaladhad
day, last of the year *n.* penninor
day, second of the week *n.* oranor
day, seventh of the week *n.* oraeron
day, sixth of the week *n.* orbelain
day, third of the week *n.* orithil
daytime *n.* arad, aur
dead *adj.* fern, gwann
dead (person) *n.* gorth II
Dead, the *n. class.pl.* gorthrim
deadly *adj.* delu
dear *adj.* mell, muin
death I *n.* gûr, gurth
death II (act of dying) *n.* gwanath, gwanu
death-horror *n.* guruthos
debate *n.* athrabeth
decagon *n.* caenthil
December *n.* girithron
decrepit (of things) *adj.* gern
deed *n.* carth
deep *adj.* nûr I
deer *n.* aras
defend *v.* gartha-

delicate *adj.* deil
deliver (from evil) *v.* edeletha-
dell *n.* im II
delving *n.* groth
demon *n.* raug
demon, great *n.* balrog
denial *n.* ubed
depart *v.* gwanna-
departed *n.* gwann
deprive *v.* neitha-
descendant *n.* inn
desert *n.* eru
desirable *adj.* írui
desire *v.* aníra-, ídhra-
desire, sexual *n.* îr
destine *v.* amartha-
determined (to do) *v.* nîdha-
detestation *n.* delos
device *n.* gaud
device, floreate *Mil.* *n.* amloth
devoted (to) *v.* dila-
devour *v.* mammada-
dew *n.* mîdh
die *v.* fir-
different *adj.* ellen
difficult (to pronounce) *adj.* dirbedui
difficult *adj.* gordh
difficulty *n.* tarias
dim *v.* gwathra-
dirty *adj.* gwaur
disguise *v.* gawa-
disgust *n.* del
disgusting *adj.* fuiol
dispute I *n.* cost
dispute II *v.* costha-
distance, remote *n.* haered
distant I *adv.* hae
distant II *adj.* haeron
distinct *adj.* minai
disturb *v.* presta-
divide *v.* ethad-
divinity *n.* balan, rodon
do *v.* car-

do (wrong) *v.* othgar-
doer *n.* ceredir
dog *n.* hû
dog, hound of chase *n.* rŷn
dome *n.* telu
doom I *n.* amarth, manadh
doom II *v.* bartha-
doomed *adj.* barad I
door *n.* fen
door, great *n.* annon
doorway *n.* fennas
dot *n.* peg
double *adj.* edaid, tadol
dough *n.* moeas
dove *n.* cugu
down, downwards *adv.* dad
downhill *adv.* dadbenn
dragon *n.* amlug
drain *v.* sautha-
draught *n.* suith
draw *v.* teitha-
draw (water) *v.* calpha-
dread *n.* achas. gae, gost
dreadful *adj.* gaer I, goeol
dream I *n.* ôl
dream II *v.* oltha-
dreamy *adj.* ólui
drear *n.* muil
dreariness *adj.* muil
drink *v.* soga-
drinking-vessel *n.* ylf
drown *v.* por-
drum *n.* labum
drunk *n.* balfaug
dry *adj.* parch
dungeon *n.* gador
Dunlendings *n.class.pl.* gwathuirim
duress *n.* thang
dusk *n.* tinnu
dusky *adj.* doll
dust *n.* ast, lith
dusty *adj.* lithui
Dwarf *n.* cadhad, hadhod, naug, nogoth

Dwarves, the *n.class.pl.* hadhodrim, gonnhirim, naugrim, nogothrim

dwell *v.* dortha-

dwelling *n.* bar

eager *adj.* bara
eagle *n.* thoron
ear *n.sing.* lhewig
earring *n.* lhewigorf
ears, pair of *n.pl.* lhaw
earth I *n.* amar, cae I
Earth II *n.* ceven
earthen *adj.* cefn
earthen-ware *n.* cefnas
ease *v.* natha-
easily *pref.* ath- II
east *n.* amrûn, rhûn, rhuven
easterlings *n.* rhúnedain
eastern *adj.* rhúnen
easy *adj.* rhae
easy, to achieve *n.* dadbenn
easy, to do *adj.* athgar
easy, to see *adj.* athgen
eat *v.* mad-
eating, gluttonous *n.* laudh
eavesdrop *v.* lathra-, lathrada-
eavesdropper *n.* lathron, lethril
ebb *n.* dannen
echo I *n.* glamor
echo II *v.* lamma-
echoing *adj.* glamren
edge *n.* rîw
edge, sharp *n.* lanc III
eel *n.* ingwil
egg *n.* ott
eight *adj.num.* toloth
eighth *adj.num.* tolthui, tolothen
elder *adj.* einior
elephant *n.* annabon
eleven *adj.num.* mimp, minib
Elf *n.* edhel, penedh
Elf, dark *n.* mornedhel
Elf-friend *n.* elvellon
Elf, Grey *n.* thinnedhel
Elf-maid *n.* elleth
Elf, male *n.* ellon
Elf, Teler *n.* teler

elf-stone *n.* edhelharn

elm-tree *n.* alaf, lalorn (arch.), lalven (arch.), lalwen (arch.)

Elven-fair *adj.* edhelvain

Elves, Green *n.class.pl.* laegrim

Elves, of Doriath *n.class.pl.* iathrim

Elves, of Lothlórien *n.class.pl.* galadhrim

Elves, Silvan *n.class.pl.* tawarwaith

Elves, Teleri *n.class.pl.* telerrim

elvish *adj.* edhellen

embers *n.* iûl

eminent *adj.* orchal

emit (foul breath) *v.* faw-

emotion *n.* felf

empty *adj.* cofen, lost

encampment *n.* estolad

enchant *v.* lútha-

enclose *v.* gleina-

enclosure, circular *n.* cerin

enclosure, fenced *n.* haedh

end I *n.* meth, methed

end II *adj.* methen

end III *v.* meth- II

endless *adj.* arnediad, aronoded

endure *v.* brenia-, dartha-

enduring *adj.* bronadui

enemy *n.* coth

enfold *v.* gwaeda-

enlaced *adj.* raen II

enlarge *v.* panna- I

enmity *n.* coth

enough *adv.* far, farn

Ent *n.* onod

entangle *v.* gonathra-

entanglement *n.* gonathras

enter *v.* minna-, neledh-

envelope *n.* ui I

Eorlingas *n.* thoronhîn

error *n.* mist, mistad

especially *adv.* edregol

establish *v.* tangada-

estuary *n.* ethir I

eternal *adj.* uireb

eternity *n.* uir

evening *n.* aduial, thîn (arch.)

ever *pref.* ui, ui- II

ever-closed *adj.* uidafnen

everybody *relative. pron.* páphen

evil *adj.* ogol, um

exalted *adj.* hall I

excavate *v.* rosta-

excavation *n.* torech

excel *v.* aria-

excellent I *adj.* maer

excellent II *interj.* ma

except *prep.* eng

exclamation, of wonder or delight *n.* elo

exile *n.* edledhron, egel

exile, go into *v.* edledhia-

exiled *adj.* edlenn

expand *v.* beltha-

extremely *adv.* íd

eye *n.* hen

eyes, of *adj.* heneb

eyes, pair of *n.* hent

face *n.* nîf, thîr
fade I *v.* gwanna-, pel- II
fade II (to grow towards evening) *v.* thinna-
fading *n.* peleth, pelin
fading, season of *n.* firith
fail *v.* dew-
faintness *n.* hwîn
fair *adj.* bain
fair (and pale) *adj.* gwân
fair-haired *adj.* baen
faith *n.* astor, bronwe
fall I *n.* dant, lant II
fall II *v.* danna-
falling *adj.* talt
falsify *v.* gawa-
family *n.* nost, nothrim
family (line, or tree) *n.* nothlir
famous *adj.* palan-hinnen
fang *n.* carch
fantastic *adj.* hwiniol
far I *adv.* hae
far II *adj.* haeron
farewell *interj. and n.* novaer
fashion *v.* echad-
fasten *v.* taetha-
fat I *n.* lar
fat II *adj.* tûg
fate *n.* amarth, manadh
fated *adj.* amarthan
father *n.* adar
fathom *n.* raew
fear I *n.* achas, del, niphred
fear II *v.* gosta-
fear, great *n.* goe
fearful *adj.* gaer I
feast *n.* mereth
feat *n.* carth
feather *n.* pess
February *n.* nínui
feel *v.* matha-
feel (disgust) *v.* fuia-
feel (emotion) *v.* fel-

feel (terror) *v.* groga-
feel (with the hand) *v.* plada-
fell *adj.* delu
female *adj.* inu
fence I *n.* iâth
fence II *v.* thora-
fence, of spikes *n.* cail
fence, outer *n.* ephel
fenland *n.* lô
festival *n.* mereth
festive *adj.* meren
fetch *v.* toltha-
fetter *n.* nadh
field *n.* parth, sant
field, fenced *n.* pêl
field, flat *n.* talf II
field, sown *n.* rîdh
fierce *adj.* braig, bregol
fierceness *n.* bregolas
fiery *adj.* bara, nórui
fifth *adj.num.*ord. lefnui, lemui
fight I *n.* maeth
fight II *v.* maetha- I
fill *v.* panna- II
filth *n.* saw II
final *adj.* methen
find *v.* hir-
find (a way to something) *v.* rada-
fine *adj.* brand, lhind, trîw
finger *n.* leber
finger, index *n.* lebdas
finger, little *n.* lebig, niged
finger, middle *n.* lebenedh
finger, ring *n.* lebent
fingers, thumb and index together *n.* nobad
finish *v.* teltha-
fire *n.* naur, ûr I
fireplace *n.* ruist
firm *adj.* tanc, taug, thand II
firmament *n.* menel
first *adj.num.* main, minui
first-voiced, verse mode of *n.* minlamad
fish *n.* hâl, lim III

fisherman *n.* limraedor
fist *n.* dond
fist, clenched *n.* drambor
fist, for holding tools *n.* paur
five *num.* leben
fix *v.* penia-
flagstone *n.* ammal
flame I *v.* lacha-
flame II *n.* naur
flame, leaping *n.* lach
flap *v.* blab-
flea *n.* cáfru
flee *v.* drega-
flesh *n.* rhaw II
flet *n.* talan
float *v.* loda-
flood *n.* duinen
flood-water *n.* iôl
floor *n.* talaf
floor, wooden *n.* panas
flour *n.* mulf
flow *v.* siria-
flow, like a torrent *v.* rib-
flow (out) *v.* ethiria-
flower I *n.* loth
flower II *v.* edlothia-
flower, golden *n.* mallos
flower, golden water *n.* ninglor
flower, single *n.* lotheg
flower, small and white (immortal) *n.* alfirin
flower, stonecrop *n.* seregon
flowers, head of *n.* goloth
flowing *n.* sirith
flowing (of water) *adj.* cell
flute *n.* sim
fly *v.* revia-
fly, large *n.* budh
fly, small *n.* idh
foam I *n.* falf, gwing
foam II *v.* faltha-
foe *n.* gûd
fog *n.* hîth, hithu
fog, white *n.* mith I

foggy *adj.* hethu, hithui
foliage *n.* golas
follow *v.* aphada-
follower *n.* aphadon, bŷr, echil
food *n.* mann
food, cooked *n.* aes
foot *n.* tâl
foot, animal's *n.* pôd
footprint *n.* rein
footstool *n.* tharas
ford *n.* athrad, iach
foresee *v.* abgen-
foresight *n.* abgen
forest *n.* taur II
forester *n.* tauron
forever *n.* anuir
forge *v.* maga-
forget *v.* dadhren-
forgive *v.* díhena-, gohena-
forked *adj.* thanc
formation (tapering to a point) *n.* naith
formed *adj.* cadu
forsake *v.* awartha-
forsaken *adj.* eglan
fort *n.* garth
forth *pref.* ed-
fortress *n.* barad II, garth
fortress, underground *n.* othronn
fortunate *adj.* alwed
fortune *n.* manadh
fountain *n.* eithel
four *num.* canad
fourth *num. adj.* canthui
fowl *n.* porog
fox *n.* rusc
fragrant *adj.* liss
frail *adj.* mîw
free *adj.* lain I
freeze *v.* hel-
frequent *adj.* laew, rem II
fresh *adj.* cîw, laeb
friend *n.* mellon, meldir, meldis
friendliness *n.* miluias

friendly *adj.* milui
friendship *n.* gwend I
frog *n.* cabor
from *prep.* o I
front *n.* nîf
frost *n.* niss
frosty *adj.* nithren
fruit *n.* iaf
full *adj.* pant
fullness *n.* pathred
fungus *n.* hwand
fur *n.* heleth, helf

gap *n.* gas

gape *v.* iag-

garden *n.* sant

garland *n.* rî

garment *n.* hamp

gash *n.* naedh

gate, great *n.* annon

gateway *n.* fennas

gather *v.* cova-

gay *adj.* meren

gaze *v.* tir-, tiria-

generous *adj.* fael I

giant *n.* noroth

giddiness *n.* hwîn

gift *n.* ant

girdle *n.* lest

girl *n.* iell

girl, in her teens *n.* neth II

give *v.* anna-

give knowledge *v.* istanna-

giver *n.* oneth

glance (at) *v.* glintha-

glass *n.* heledh

gleam *n.* glîn

glimmering *adj.* gael

glint I *n.* glîn

glint II *v.* tinna-

glisten *v.* thilia-

glittering *n.* galad

glittering (white) *adj.* silivren

globe *n.* coron

globed *adj.* corn

gloom *n.* daw, fuin, maur

gloomy *adj.* dem, dofen

glorify *v.* egleria-

glorious *adj.* aglareb

glory *n.* claur

glory, great *n.* aglar

gluttonous *adj.* madweg

go *v.* gwa-, men- III

gobble (up) *v.* mammada-

goblet *n.* sûl II

gold, metal *n.* côl, malt
golden *adj.* mallen
Gondolin, people of *n.class.pl.* Gondolindrim
good I *adj.* maer
good II *interj.* ma
goodness *n.* maeras
goose *n.* gwaun
gooseberry *n.* melph
gorge *n.* cîl I
gorge, deep *n.* cabed
gorge (on) *v.* mammada-
grade *n.* tell
grandchild *n.* inn
grasp *v.* maba-
grass *n.* glae
grass, stiff *n.* thâr
grassland, wide *n.* nan
grave I *adj.* úlal
grave II *n.* haudh, sarch
gravel *n.* brith
grease *n.* lar
great *adj.* beleg, daer I
greedy *adj.* melch
green *adj.* calen
green (and fresh) *adj.* laeg II (arch.)
greet *v.* suila-, suilanna-
greeting *n.* suil, suilad
grey *adj.* thinn
grey, of *adj.* mithren
grey (pale) *adj.* mith II
grind *v.* run-
gross (144) *adj.num.* host
ground *n.* talaf
growth *n.* galas
guard *v.* tir-, tiria-
guarded *pp.* tirnen
guess I *n.* inc
guess II *v.* inga-
guest *n.* nathal
guesthouse *n.* sennas
guilty *adj.* crumguru
gulf *n.* iâ, iau II
gull *n.* gwael, maew, mŷl

gull, small *n.* cuen

habit *n.* haew
hack (through) *v.* hasta-
hair, braided *n.* finnel
hair, lock of *n.* fing
hair, ringlet of *n.* laws
hair, shaggy *n.* fast
half I *pref.* per-
half II *n.* perin
Half-Elf *n.* peredhel
hall *n.* tham
hall, great *n.* thamas
hallow *v.* aina-
halt *n.* post
hammer I *n.* dam, dring
hammer II *v.* damma-
hams *n.* hach
hand *n.* cam, maw I (arch.)
hand, left *n.* crum, hair, harvo
hand, right *n.* feir, forvo
hand-full *n.* mâb
handle *v.* maetha- II, matha-
handy *adj.* maed II
hang *v.* glinga-
harass *v.* trasta-
harbour *n.* hûb, lorn
harbourage *n.* hobas
hard *adj.* norn
hare *n.* laboth
harp *n.* gannel
harper *n.* talagan
hasty *adj.* celeg
hat *n.* carab
hateful *adj.* delu
have (to hold) *v.* gar-
have (to possess) *v.* saf-
haven *n.* círbann, hûb
havens *n.* lonnath
hawk *n.* fion
head *n.* dôl
headland *n.* ness
heal *v.* nesta-
healing *adj.* nestadren

heap *n.* cum, ovras

hear *v.* lar-

heart I (in the moral sense) *n.* gûr I

heart II (physical) *n.* hûn

hearth *n.* ruist

heat *n.* ûr I

heat, white *n.* brass I

heave *v.* amortha-

heaven, high *n.* menel

heavy *adj.* long

hedge *n.* cai

hedge, of spikes *n.* caraes

height *n.* hallas

heir *n.* arion, hîl

heirloom *n.* advîr

Hell *n.* Udûn

helm *n.Mil.* thôl

helmet *n.* harn III

help *v.* natha-

helpful *adj.* nathaweg

hem *n.* glân II, rîw

heptagon *n.* odothil

herb *n.* salab

here *adv.* si

hero *n.* callon, thalion

hew *v.* drava-

hexagon *n.* enethil

hide *v.* tor-

hidden *adj.* hall II, thurin

hideous *adj.* uanui

high *adj.* hall I

high, in size *adj.* brand, taer II

hill *n.* amon, dôl, tund

hill, isolated with a watchtower *n.* mindon

historical *adj.* gobennathren

history *n.* gobennas, pennas

Hobbit *n.* perian

Hobbits, the *n.* periannath

holder *n.* taew

hole *n.* dath, gas, torech

hole, fine pierced *n.* tess

hollow *adj.* coll II, raudh

hollow (out) *v.* rosta-

holly *n.* ereg
holly, the land of *n.* eregion
holly-tree *n.* eregdos
holy *adj.* aer II
home *n.* bar
home, dear *n.* milbar
homeland *n.* bardor
honey *n.* glî
honeycomb *n.* nîdh
hook *n.* gamp
hop *v.* laba-
hope I *n.* estel
hope II *v.* hartha-
hope, based on reason *n.* amdir
horde *n.* hoth
horizon *n.* meneldaeg
horn I *n.* rass, tarag, till
horn II *n.* rom
horns, sound of *n.* romru
horrible *adj.* deleb, gortheb
horror *n.* del, girith, gorog, goroth
horror, extreme *n.* gorgor
horse, for riding *n.* roch
horse, for working *n.* lobor
horse-lord *n.* rochir
Horse-Lords *n.class.pl.* rochirrim
host *n.* hoth, rim I
hot *adj.* born, urui
hour *n.* lu
house *n.* adab, car
household *n.* herth
how *interrogative.pron.* manen
human *n.* firen
hummock *n.* gwastar
hump *n.* tump
hundred, one *num.* haran
hungry *adj.* saig
hunt I *v.* fara-
hunt II *n.* rui
hunter *n.* feredir
hunter, male *n.* faron
hunters *n.* faradrim, faroth
hunting *n.* faras

hurl *v.* had-
husband *n.* benn, hervenn
hyacinth *n.* lingui

ice *n.* heleg
icicle *n.* aeglos
icy *adj.* helegren
idea *n.* inc, naw
identical *adj.* imu
idle *adj.* úgar
idling *adj.* úgarol
if *conj.* pe
ignorant *v.* gwista-
ill *adj.* lhaew II
Ilúvatar *n.* iladar
image *n.* emm
imagination *n.* ing
immortal *adj.* alfirin
impelled *adj.* horn
impetus *n.* gorf
impetuous *adj.* alag, asgar, gorn
imprison *adj.* gadoras
impulse *n.* felf
in I *prep.* mi
in II *pref.* nedh-
in, during *prep.* ned
incline *n.* talad
ink *n.* mûr
innocence *n.* glanas
innumerable *adj.* arnediad, aronoded
insane *adj.* penind
insecure *adj.* talt
insert *v.* nestag-
instead *adv.* sennui
insult *v.* eitha-
intelligence *n.* hannas
intelligent *adj.* hand
intend *v.* thel-
interact *v.* athragar-
interaction *n.* athragardh
into *prep.* mina
iris *n.* palath II
iron *n.* ang
iron, of *adj.* angren
island *n.* tol
isle (flat) *n.* caer

isolated *adj.* ereb
ivy *n.* ethil

January *n.* narwain
jaw *n.* anc, carach. naew
jerk I *n.* rinc
jerk II *v.* ritha-
jewel *n.* mîr
jewel-smith *n.* mírdan
joke *n.* cag
journey I *v.* ledh-
journey II *n.* lend I
journey-bread *n.* lembas
joy *n.* gell, glass
joyful *adj.* gellweg
joyous *adj.* gellui, glassui, meren
jubilation *n.* gellam
judge I *v.* badh-
judge II *n.* badhor
judgement *n.* baudh
juice *n.* paich, saw
juicy *adj.* pihen
July *n.* ceveth
June *n.* nórui
just *adj.* fael I
justice *n.* faelas

keen *adj.* laeg I
keenness *n.* laegnas
keep *v.* heb-
Khazad-Dûm *n.* dornhabar
kind *adj.* milui
kindle *v.* nartha-
kindler *n.* thoniel
kindliness *n.* miluias
kindred *n.* nost
king *n.* aran, âr, taur I
kingdom *n.* arnad
kingfisher *n.* heledir
kingsfoil *n.* athelas
kinsman *n.* gwanur
kiss *v.* mib-
knead *v.* maega-
knife *n.* sigil I
knight *n.* arben
knob, round *n.* dolt
knock *v.* tamma-
knot *n.* nardh
knotted *adj.* norn
know *v.* ista-
knowledge *n.* ist

laborious *adj.* gordh

labour I *v.* muda-

labour II *n.* tass

lacking *adj.* penna

lady *n.* brennil, dî, heryn, hiril

lair *n.* caew, torech

lake *n.* ael

lake, cold (in the mountains) *n.* rim II

lake, shallow *n.* lô

lamb *n.* iol

lament, woeful *n.* naergon

lamentable *adj.* naer

lamentation *n.* conath, nírnaeth

lamp, portable *n.* calar

lampwright *n.* calardan

lancer *n.* rohaith

land *n.* dôr

land, central *n.* ennor

land, flat *n.* talf II

land, foreign *n.* ethel

land, inhabited *n.* bar

language *n.* lam II

lapis lazuli *n.* ningon

large *adj.* beleg

last I *v.* brona-

last II *adj.* medui

lasting *adj.* bronadui

later *prep. pref.* ab-

laugh *v.* gladh-, lala-

laughter *n.* lalaith

law *n.* thann

lay, long (poem) *n.* glaer

lead *v.* tog-

lead (out) *v.* ethog-

leaf *n.* lass

league *n.* daur

lean *adj.* lhain

leap *v.* cab-

learn *v.* gelia-

learned *adj.* istui

learned, in deep arts *adj.* golwen

left *n.* crom

left-handed *adj.* crumui, hargam

letter *n.* têw

level *adj.* land I

lick *v.* lav-

lie *v.* fur-

lie (down) *v.* caeda-

lie (heavy) *v.* dufa-

life *n.* cuil

lifetime *n.* lúguil

lift *v.* hal-

light I *n.* calad, galad

light II *adj.* lim II

light, bright *n.* gail

light, golden *n.* glawar

light, golden of Laurelin *n.* glaur

like I *v.* sera-

like II *conj.* sui

lily *n.* inil

limit I *v.* gleina-

limit II *n.* taeg

line *n.* tê, tî

link *n.* lif

lion *n.* raw II

lip *n.* pé

listen *v.* lasta-

little *adj.* pîn, tithen

live *v.* cuia-

load *n.* cûl

loaf *n.* basgorn

loathing *n.* del, delos

loathsome *adj.* deleb

lode *n.* rant

lofty *adj.* brand, orchal, taer II

log, hewn *n.* drafn

lonely *adj.* ereb

long *adj.* and

long (and thin) *adj.* taen II

long, for a long time *adv.* Anann

Longbeard *n. sing.* anfang

Longbeards *n. pl.* anfangrim

long-mark *n.* andaith

long-shorts *n. pl.* ann-thennath

long-suffering *adj.* andreth

long (sight) *n.* foen
look I *n.* thîr
look (towards) II *v.* tir-
loom *v.* brasta-
loose, let loose *v.* adleg-
lord *n.* brannon, hîr
lore *n.* ist
lore, deep *n.* angol
lore, magic *n.* gûl
lore-master *n.* pengolodh
Lórien *n.* olfannor
lose *v.* danhir-
loud *adj.* brui
louse *n.* gwef
love I *v.* dila-, mela-
love II *n.* meleth, mîl
lovely *adj.* melui
lover *n.* melethor, melethril, melethron, seron
loving *adj.* milui
low *adj.* tofen
lowlying *adj.* tofen
loyal *adj.* sador
loyalty *n.* astor
lust *n.* mael II
lustful *adj.* maelui
lyre *n.* salf

machine *n.* gaud
magic *n.* angol
magician *n.* gollor
maiden *n.* gwend II
make *v.* echad-
make firm *v.* tangada-
make ready *v.* feria-
maker *n.* ceredir
male I *n.* benn
male II *adj.* anu
Man, the fathers of *n. sing.* adanadar
Man, the race of *n.* adan
man *n.* benn, dîr (arch.)
man, one-handed *n.* erchammon
man, mortal *n.* firion
man, wild *n.* rhavan
manage *v.* maetha- II
Mandos *n.* bannos, gurfannor
manhood *n.* gwaith
mantle *n.* coll III
Manwë *n.* aran einior
many *adj.* odrim
marble *n.* glast
March *n.* gwaeron
mark *n.* tagol, taith
market-place *n.* bahad
marriage *n.* best
marry *v.* besta-
master 1 *n.* herdir, heron, hîr
master II *v.* orthor-
mastery *n.* tûr
marvellous *adj.* elvennui
mathematics *n.* gonodvaeras
May *n.* lothron
mayor *n.* condir
mead *n.* enn
meagre *adj.* lhain
mean I *adj.* faeg
mean II *v.* thel-
meat *n.* aes
meet *v.* cova-, covad-
memory *n.* rínas

Men, all of the *n.* class *pl.* adanath
Mercury *n.* gilvír
mere *n.* ael
mesh *n.* rem I
metal *n.* raud, tinc
metal, black *n.* galvorn
mid *pref.* nedh-
middle *n.* ened
middle-earth *n.* ennor, ennorath
mighty *adj.* belaith, beleg, taur III
milk, to turn *v.* curtha-
millennium *n.* andrann
mine *n.* fela
mine, delved *n.* sabar
mirror *n.* cenedril
misdeed *n.* othgarn
miss *v.* dew-
mist *n.* hîth
mist, wet *n.* mith I
mistake *n.* dŷl
mistaken *adj.* dŷr
mistaken act *adj.* dýgar
mist-thread *n.* hithlain
misty *adj.* hithui
mocking *n.* iaew
moisten *v.* limmida-
monster *n.* úan, ulunn
monstrous *adj.* uanui
moon *n.* ithil
moon, crescent *n.* cúron
moon, new *n.* cýron
morning, early *n.* arduil
morrowdim *n.* minuial
mortal I *n.* fair I
mortal II *adj.* fireb
moth *n.* mal
mother *n.* emel, emil, naneth
mound *n.* cerin, coron, cum, tund
mountain *n.* dôl, orod
mountaineer *n.* orodben
mountain peak *n.* aegas, tarag
mountain peaks, range of *n.* aeglir
mountains, range of *n.* menniath

mouth *n.* nóf

move *v.* men- III

move (sudden) *n.* rinc

mud *n.* madh

mummy, mommy *n.*dim. nana

murmur *n.* norr

muscle *n.* tû

music *n.* gling

mutated, of vowels *pp.* prestannen

mutation, of vowels *n.* prestanneth

nail *n.* taes
naked *adj.* hell, lanc I, paran, parch II
name I *n.* eneth
name II *v.* esta-
Nandor *n.* danwaith
narrator *n.* pethron
narrow *adj.* agor
nasty *adj.* oer
Nazgûl *n.* úlaer
neat *adj.* puig
neck *n.* iaeth
neck (vertebrae) *n.* achad
necklace *n.* sigil II
necromancy *n.* gûl, morgul
need I *n.* baur, thang
need II *v.* boe
needle *n.* nelf
neighbour *n.* sammar
neighbours, pair of *n.* samarad
nest *v.* uitha-
net *n.* gwî, rem I
netted *adj.* raen II, remmen
new *adj.* cîw, eden, gwain, sain
news *n.* siniath
next *adv.* tha, thá
nickname *n.* abeneth
night *n.* dû, môr
night, dead of *n.* fuin
nightfall *n.* dû
nightingale *n.* dúlinn, merilin
nightshade *n.* dúath
night-time *n.* daw
nimble *adj.* legol
nine *adj.num.* neder
ninth *adj.num.* nedrui
no I *pref.* al- I (arch.), ú
no II *interj.* baw
nobility *n.* arodas
noble I *adj.* arod, brand
noble II *n.* arben
noise *n.* lhôn
noise, confused *n.* glam

noise, rushing or roaring *v.* lausta-

noisy *adj.* brui

Noldo *n.* lachenn

Noldo (exiled) *n.* aredhel, gódhel

nonagon *n.* nederthil

noon *n.* enedhor

noose *n.* nŷw

north *n.* forn, forod, forven

northern *adj.* forodren

Northmen *n.class.pl.* forodrim, forodwaith

nose *n.* bund, nem

not *pref.* al- I (arch.), ú

notion *n.* inc

November *n.* hithui

now *adv.* thî

number, great *n.* lae

Númenórean *n.* dúnadan

numerous *adj.* rem II

nut *n.* breth, cot

O

O! *interj.* a! II
oak-tree *n.* doron
oath *n.* gwaedh, gwest
oats *n.* ruthol
oblique *adj.* adlant
obscure I *adj.* doll, hethu
obscure II *v.* gwathra-
obstinate *adj.* balthand, tarlanc
ocean *n.* aearon, gaearon
octagon *n.* tolothil
October *n.* narbeleth
odour *n.* ûl
of (from) *prep.* o I
oil *n.* mill
old *adj.* brûn, gern (of things), iaur
old-age *adj.* ingem
old-young *adj.* iarwain
on *prep.* am, bo
on (this side of) *prep.* nef
once *n.* minlû
one I *adj.num.* mîn
one II *relative.pron.* pen II
one-handed *adj.* erchamion, erchammui
onion *n.* nínholch
open I *v.* edra-, panna- I
open II *adj.* laden
oppress *v.* baugla-
oppressive *adj.* baug
oppressor *n.* bauglir
or *conj.* egor
orange I *n.* culf
orange II *adj.* cull
orange tree *n.* culforn
Orc *n.* glam, glamog, orch, urug (arch.)
Orcs *n.pl.* glamhoth, orchoth
original *adj.* iaur
Orion *n.* menelvagor
Oromë *n.* aran tauron, araw
Ossë *n.* Yssion
out *pref.* ed-
outline *n.* cant
outcry *n.* caun I

outsider *n.* edlon
oven *n.* bothil
overshadow *v.* gwathra-
overwhelming *adj.* taur III
owl *n.* hô

pain I *n.* naeg
pain, to cause II *v.* naegra
Palantir *n.* gwachaedir
pale *adj.* gael, maidh, malu, nimp I
palisade, of spikes *n.* cail
pallor *n.* niphred
palm, of hand *n.* camlann, plad, talf I
pansy *n.* helin
parchment *n.* fadhu
parent *n.* odhril, odhron, onnor
pass, between high walls *n.* aglonn
pass, in mountains *n.* dîn II, imrad
pasture *n.* nadhor, nadhras
path *n.* râd
path, narrow *n.* lond
pathway *n.* bâd
patience *n.* andreth
pause *n.* daur, post
peace *n.* sîdh
peak *n.* egnas
pea-pod *n.* eredhui
pearl *n.* aearvír
pebble *n.* sarn
pebble bank *n.* serni
pedlar *n.* bachor
peel *v.* par-
pen *n.* tegil, tegol
penis *n.* gwîb
pentagon *n.* lebthil
people (of one kind or origin) *n.* lî
perceive *v.* cen-
permission *n.* dâf
permit *v.* daf-
person, faithful *n.* sador, sadron
person, wicked *n.* ogron
petal *n.* lothlas
petrel *n.* cuen
petty *adj.* niben
pick up (with the fingers) *v.* leutha-
picture *n.* emm
piercing *adj.* maeg
pig *n.* pholg

pile (of rock or earth) *n.* mâf
pilgrim *n.* randir
pillar, wooden *n.* thafn
pillow *n.* pesseg
pin *n.* tachol
pine-tree *n.* thôn
pink *adj.* crinth
pipe *n.* sim
pipe-weed *n.* galenas
pippin *n.* cordof
pit *n.* dath
pivot *n.* pelthaes
place *n.* sad
place, holy *n.* iaun
place, of work *n.* mudathad
plank *n.* pân I
plant *n.* galas
platform, wooden (in the trees) *n.* talan
play I *v.* telia-
play II *n.* telien
play (a harp) *v.* ganna-, gannada-
please *v.* fasta-
Pleiades *n.* remmirath
poem *n.* glîr
poem, narrative *n.* glaer
poet *n.* maeron
point I *n.* aeg, ment, till
point II *v.* nasta-
point, of spear *n.* thela
point, sharp *n.* egnas, nass
poison *n.* saew
polish *v.* run-
pollen *n.* mâl
ponder *v.* idhra-
pondering *adj.* idhren
ponderous *adj.* grond
pool *n.* ael, lîn, loeg
pool, cold (in the mountains) *n.* rim II
pool, small *n.* both
pools *n.* liniath
poor *adj.* faeg
poplar-tree *n.* tulus
porridge *n.* ruthol

possess *v.* saf-
post *n.* tagol
potato *n.* ceforf
potter *n.* cennan
pottery *n.* cefnas
praise *v.* daetha-, egleria-
pray *v.* her-
precipice *n.* avras, rhass
pregnant *n.* gaiw
preserve (in memory) *v.* ephola-
prick *v.* ercha-, nasta-
prick, with sharp point *v.* eitha-
prickle *n.* erch
pride *n.* tarlangas
prince *n.* arion, caun III, cund (arch.), ernil
princess *n.* aranel, ariel
prison *n.* band, gador
prisoner *n.* gadorphen
private *adj.* said
prize *v.* idra-
prohibit *v.* boda-
prop *n.* tulu
property *n.* garn
prosper (cause to) *v.* alia-
prosperous *adj.* alwed
protect *v.* beria-
proud *adj.* tarlanc
province *n.* ardhon
puddle *n.* both
puff I *n.* hwest
puff II *v.* hwesta-
purity *n.* glanas
purple *adj.* ling
putrescence *n.* saw II
putrid (of food) *adj.* saur

Q

quadrilateral *n.* canthil
quarrel I *n.* cost
quarrel II *v.* costha-
quarter *n.* canath
queen *n.* bereth, rîn I, rîs
quench *v.* luithia-
Quenya *n.* golodhbaeth
quickly *adv.* lim I
quiet *adj.* tîn II

R

rabbit *n.* laboth
race (on horses) *v.* northa-
race (of people) *n.* nûr II
race, riding *n.* north
radiance *n.* galad, gal-, glaw
radiant *n.* faen
rage I *n.* oroth
rage II *v.* ruthra-
rain I *n.* ross I
rain II *v.* elia-
rainbow *n.* eiliant, ninniach
raindrop *n.* rosseg
rainy *adj.* rost
raise *v.* ortha-
range *n.* lîr I
ransom *n.* danwedh
rape *v.* maitha-
rapid *adj.* lagor
rat *n.* nâr
rather *adv.* sennui
raven *n.* craban
ravine *n.* cirith, falch, iau II, riss
ravish *v.* maitha-
reach (for) *v.* raitha-
read (silently, to oneself) *v.* henna-
read (written material) *v.* tengwa-
readiness (for action) *n.* hûr
ready (to hand) *adj.* ferui
realm *n.* ardh
reap *v.* critha-
rear *n.* tele
recite (a poem) *v.* glir-
reckon *v.* genedia-, gonod-
recount *v.* trenar-
red *adj.* caran, naru
red, fiery *adj.* ruin
red, golden *adj.* coll I
red-haired *adj.* ross II
reed *n.* lisg
reek *n.* osp
refill *v.* adbanna-
reflection *n.* galad

refresh *v.* cytha-
refusal *n.* avad
refusal, gesture with the hand *n.* ablad
refuse *v.* ava-
refuser *n.* avar
regiment *n.* gwaith
region *n.* ardh
region, bounded or defined *n.* gardh
rejoice *v.* gella-
release I *v.* adleg- (arch.), adleitha-, leithia-
release II *n.* leithian
reluctance *n.* avad
remain *v.* dar-, dartha-
remember *v.* ephola-, ren-
remembrance *n.* rín II
remote I *adv.* hae
remote II *n.* haered
rename *v.* adesta-
rend *v.* narcha-, rista-
renew *v.* cytha-
renewal *n.* cîl II
renewed *adj.* cîr
rephrase *v.* adbed-
reply I *n.* dangweth
reply II *v.* aphed-
report *n.* gweth
resin *n.* thuith
resonant *adj.* tong
rescue *v.* natha-
rest I *n.* îdh, post, senn
rest II *v.* posta-
resting-place *n.* caew
restless *adj.* penídh
retain *v.* heb-
return *v.* dadwen-, dananna-
reunite *v.* adertha-
reveal *v.* tengia-
revered *adj.* gorn II
ride *v.* nor-
rider, of a horse *n.* rochben, rochon
ridge *n.* pind
ridges *n.* pinnath
right I *n.* forn

right II *adj.* tîr
right-handed *adj.* forgam
rigid *adj.* tharn
ring *n.* cor
ring, outer *n.* echor
ringing (of bells) *n.* nelladel
ringlet *n.* loch
rip *v.* rista-
rise *v.* eria-
Rivendell *n.* imladris
river *n.* celon, sîr
river, great *n.* sirion
river, long and large *n.* duin
riverbank *n.* duirro, raw I
riverbed *n.* rant, rath
road *n.* men
road, paved *n.* othlonn
roaring *adj.* râf
rock *n.* gond
roof I *v.* orthel-, toba-
roof II *n.* tobas
roof, high *n.* telu
roof, of a cave (or vaulted/arched) *n.* rond
room *n.* sam
root *n.* thond
root, edible *n.* solch
rope *n.* raph
rose *n.* meril
rotten *adj.* thaur
round *adj.* corn
row *n.* lîr I, tî
royal *adj.* arnen
rub *v.* run-
ruby *n.* naruvir
ruddy *adj.* crann, gaer II, gruin
rule I *v.* bal-
rule II *n.* thann
ruler *n.* caun III
run *v.* nor-
rune *n.* certh
running *adj.* cell
running-free *adj.* legol
rushing *adj.* alag, asgar

russet *adj.* rhosc
rustling (sound) *n.* lhoss, rhoss

s-sign *n.* gammas
sad *adj.* dem, naer, nûr III
saddle *n.* rogol
sadness *n.* naeras
safe *adj.* barn
safe-keeping *n.* band
saga *n.* narn
sail *v.* cira-, revia-
sailor *n.* cirion
salt *n.* sing
salty *adj.* singren
salve *n.* glaew
same *adj.* imu
sanctuary *n.* iaun
sand *n.* lith
sap *n.* thuith
sapphire *n.* lûl
sate *v.* fadra-
save I *prep.* eng
save II *v.* natha-
saving *n.* edraith
say *v.* ped-
scarlet *adj.* coll I
scorn I *v.* eitha-
scorn II *n.* iaew
scratch *v.* rhib-
screen I *n.* esgal
screen II *v.* haltha-
sculptor *n.* gomaeron
sea *n.* aear, gaear
sea-bird *n.* cuen
sea-serpent *n.* limlug
seashell *n.* half
seaweed *n.* gaeruil, uil
second *adj.num.* edwen, tadui
second (in command) *adj.* taid
secret *adj.* thurin
sedge *n.* lisg
seduce *v.* meltha-
see *v.* cen-, tíra-
seed *n.* cot, eredh
seedpod *n.* eredhui

seek *v.* cesta-
seem *v.* thia-
select *v.* caw-
send *v.* mentha-
sensible *adj.* noen
sentence *n.* gobeth
separate *adj.* riss, said
September *n.* ivanneth
serious *adj.* úlal
serpent *n.* lhûg
serve *v.* buia-
set *v.* penia-
set aside *v.* seidia-
seven *adj.num.* odog
seventh *adj.num.* othui
sex *n.* huith
shade *n.* gwath, lum
shadow *n.* dae, dúath, gwath
shadow, of objects *n.* morchant
shadowed *adj.* hall II
shadowy *adj.* gwathren, gwathui
shady *adj.* hall II, lumren
shape *n.* cant
shaped *adj.* cadu
shapely *adj.* cadwor, maed I
shaping *n.* cannas
share *v.* ethad-
sharp *adj.* laeg I, maeg
sharp-eyed *adj.* maecheneb
sharp-pointed *adj.* megor
sharpness *n.* laegnas
sharp-sighted (with the mind) *adj.* fergenol
shatter *v.* ractha-
shave *v.* thas-
shaven *adj.* paran
sheep *n.* bá
shield *n.Mil.* thand I
shield-fence *n.Mil.* thangail
shine (clear) *v.* gal-
shine (white) *v.* síla-
shingle *n.* serni
ship *n.* cair
shipbuilder *n.* círdan

shire *n.* trann
Shire, of the *adj.* trannail
shirt *n.* laub
shoe *n.* habad
shore *n.* esgar
short *adj.* estent, then, thent
shout *v.* can-
shouting *n.* glam
shrine *n.* alchor
shudder *v.* gir-
shuddering *n.* girith
shush *interj.* sus
sick *adj.* caeleb, lhaew II
sickle *n.* cerch
sickly *adj.* gem, lhaew II
sickness *n.* cael, lhîw, paw
side, left-hand *n.* harvo
side, right-hand *n.* forvo
sign *n.* tann
signal-fire *n.* narthan
silence *n.* dîn I
silent *adj.* dínen
Silmaril *n.* golovir, mirion, silevril
silver *n.* celeb
silver, like *adj.* celebren
simbelmynë *n.* uilos
similar *adj.* gonef
sin *n.* úgarth
Sinda *n.* Thinnedhel
Sindar *n.class.pl.* Thindrim
sinew *n.* tû
sing *v.* glir-, linna-, liria-
single *adj.* er, erui, minai
sinister *adj.* crumguru
sinner *n.* raegdan
Sirius *n.* helluin
sister *n.* neth II, nethel
sister, dear *n.* muinthel
sister, sworn *n.* gwathel
sit *v.* haf-
six *adj.num.* eneg
sixth *adj.num.* enchui, enegui
skilful *adj.* maed II

skill *n.* curu

skilled *adj.* maed II, maen

skin *n.* flâd

skull *n.* cas

sky *n.* eil, menel

slant *v.* adlanna-

slant, downwards *v.* penna-

slanting *adj.* adlant

slash *n.* criss

slave *n.* mûl

slay *v.* dag-

slayer *n.* dagnir

sleep *v.* losta-

slender *adj.* fim, lhind, nind, trîw

slim *adj.* fim

sling *n.Mil.* hadlath

slipping *adj.* talt

slope I *v.* adlanna-

slope II *n.* pend, talad

sloping *adj.* adlann

small *adj.* cidinn, cinnog, mîw, niben

small (and frail) *adj.* nimp II

smell *n.* thost

smell (something) *v.* nosta-

smith *n.* tân

smoke I *n.* osp

smoke II *v.* ospa-

smooth I *adj.* paran, path

smooth II *v.* patha-

snake *n.* lhûg, lŷg

sneeze *v.* hedia-

snout *n.* bund

snouted *adj.* bon

snow I *n.* loss

snow II *v.* glosta-

snowdrop *n.* nínim, niphredil

snowflake *n.* lossivor

Snowmen (of Forochel) *n.class.pl.* lossoth

Snowthorn *n.* aeglos

snow-white *adj.* gloss

snowy *adj.* lossen

soaking (wet) *adj.* loen

soap *n.* glûdh

socket *n.* taew
soft *adj.* moe
soften *v.* maega-
soil *n.* cef
soiled *adj.* gwaur
soldier, of orcs *n.* daug
sole (of foot) *n.* tellen
sombre *adj.* dûr
someone *relative pron.* pen II
son *n.* ion
song *n.* glîr, laer II
song, great *n.* beleglinn
song, holy *n.* aerlinn
songwriter *n.* glirvaeron
sorcery, dark *n.* guldur, morgul
soul *n.* fae
sound *n.* lhôn
sound (bells) *v.* nella-
sound, loud (of trumpets) *n.* rû
soup *n.* salph
source *n.* celu
south *n.* harad, harn I
southern *adj.* haradren
Southerners *n.class.pl.* haradrim
south-region *n.* harven
sow *v.* redh-
space, open *adj.* land I
spark *n.* tin, tint
spark, bright *n.* gil
spark, silver *n.* gildin
spark, small star *n.* tint
sparkle I *n.* tin
sparkle (like a jewel) II *v.* míria-
sparkling *adj.* lim II
sparkling (like a jewel) *adj.* míriel
speak *v.* ped-
speak (about something continuously) *n.* himannol
spear-point *n.* aith, ecthel
spear-thrower *n.* hador, hadron
spectre, vague *n.* auth II
speech *n.* paeth
speech, barbarous *n.* glam
speed (on) *v.* hortha-

spell *n.* lûth
spelling *n.* téwgiled
spider *n.* lhing, lhingril, ungol
spike *n.* carag, ceber
spin-drift *n.* gwing
spine *n.* ech
spinning wheel *n.* cerf
spirit *n.* faer
spirit, departed *n.* mân
spirit, fiery *n.* hûr
spit *v.* puia-
splendour *n.* aglar, claur (arch.)
split *adj.* thanc
sponge *n.* hwand
spoor *n.* rein
sport *n.* telien
spot, small *n.* peg
spouse, of a king *n.* bereth
spread *v.* pelia-
spring I *n.* celu, eithel
Spring II *n.* ethuil
spring III *v.* tuia-
Spring, beginning of *n.* echuir
sprout I *v.* tuia-
sprout II *n.* tui
spy *n.* ethir II
stab *v.* eitha-
staff *n.Mil.* fannil
stain I *n.* gwass, mael I, maw II
stain II *v.* gwatha-
stained *adj.* gwaen, mael I
stairway *n.* pendrath
stake *n.* ceber
stalwart *adj.* thala, tolog
standard *n.* tull
star *n.* êl, geil
star, small *n.* tint
starlight *n.* gilgalad
stars, all of the *n.* elenath, giliath
star-sun, flower *n.* elanor
startle *v.* cautha-
stay *v.* dar-, dartha-, dortha-
staying, fast *adj.* avorn

steadfast *adj.* him I, sador
steady *adj.* thala
steel *n.* gais
steel, of *adj.* gaithren
steep *adj.* baradh
steeple *n.* brand II
stem *n.* telch
stench *n.* ongol, thû
step I *v.* pad-
step II *n.* pâd
step (in a stairway or ladder) *n.* tell
stick *v.* himia-
sticky *adj.* hîw
stiff *adj.* dorn, tara, tarch, tharn
stiff-necked *adj.* tarlanc
stiffness *n.* tarias
still *adv.* eno
stink *v.* thosta-
stirrup *n.* talraph
stone (as a material) *n.* sarn
stone, great *n.* gond
stone, hewn *n.* gondrafn, gondram
stone, made of *adj.* gondren
stone, small *n.* sarn
stop I *v.* dar-
stop II *n.* daur
stop-gap (diacritic sign) *n.* gasdil
stopped *adj.* hollen
stopper *n.* dîl
stop-up *v.* dilia-
storm, of wind *n.* alagos
straight *adj.* taer, tîr
straightness *n.* tíras
strange *adj.* ellen
stranger *n.* edlon, othol
stray *v.* mista-, renia-
straying *n.* mistad
stream *n.* celeth
stream, mountain *n.* oll
street *n.* othrad, rath
strength, bodily *n.* bellas
strip *v.* heltha-
strive *v.* raitha-

stroke *v.* matha-
stroke, heavy *n.* dram
strong *adj.* taug
strong (in body) *adj.* belt
struggle, uphill *adv. adj.* ambenn
stuffing *n.* dîl
stunt *v.* nuitha-
stunted *adj.* naug
sublime *adj.* bereth
sudden *adj.* bragol, bregol
suddenness *n.* breged
suffice *v.* feira-
sufficient *adv.* far
sugar *n.* glist
summer *n.* laer I
summit (of a high mountain) *n.* taen I
summon *v.* toltha-
sum up *v.* gonod-
sun *n.* anor
sun, light of/heat of *n.* ast II
sunken *adj.* dúven
sunlight *n.* aur, glawar
sunshine *n.* glaw
sunny *adj.* nórui
sunset *n.* annûn
superior *adj.* orchal
support *n.* tulu
supreme *adj.* bereth
surface *n.* palath
surface, flat *n.* talath
surpass *v.* latha-
survive *v.* brona-
swallow I (bird) *n.* tuilinn
swallow II (the action of) *n.* nu-laf
swan *n.* alph
sward *n.* parth, pathu
swart *adj.* baran, donn, grau
swarthy *adj.* donn
swear *v.* gwesta-
sweat *n.* fládvídh
sweep *v.* hwertha-
sweet I *adj.* lend II, melui
sweet II *adj.* laich

148

sweetly *adv.* lendren
swell *v.* tuia-
swift I *adj.* celeg, lagor
swift II *adv.* lim I
swooping *adj.* thôr
sword *n.Mil.* crist, lang, megil
swordsman *n.Mil.* magor
sympathy *n.* gofelf
syrup *n.* paich

table *n.* sarf

tail *n.* pim

take *v.* maba-

tale *n.* narn, pent, trenarn

tale, novel *n.* sinnarn

talk *v.* carfa-

talkative *adj.* pedweg

tall *adj.* taer II, tond

tangled *adj.* remmen

task *n.* tass

tassel *n.* fath

taste *v.* caw-, taf-

taut *adj.* tong

tea *n.* suithlas

teach *v.* goltha-, istanna-

tear *n.* nîn II, nîr

tearful *adj.* nîd, níniel

tease (wool) *v.* tûs-

tell (to the end) *v.* trenar-

temple *n.* alchor

teeth, all of the *n.* naglath

teeth, row of *n.* carach

tell (a tale) *v.* nara- (arch.)

Telperion *n.* galathil

temptation *n.* úthaes

ten *num.* cae II

tenth *adj.* caenen, caenui

terrify *v.* gruitha-

terrifying *adj.* goeol

terror *n.* goe, gorgor

thank *v.* hanna-

thankful *adj.* hannweg

thatch *n.* taus

the I *art.pron.rel.sing.* i,

the II *art.pron.rel.pl.* in

then *adv.* tha, thá

there *adv.* dha, ennas

thick *adj.* tûg

thigh *n.* tûd

thin *adj.* lhain

thing *n.* nad

thing (made by handicraft) *n.* tafen

think *v.* sam-
third I *adj.num.* nail, nelui
third II *n.* nelest
thirsty *adj.* faug
thirtieth *adj.num.* nelchaenen
thong, leather *n.* lath
thorn *n.* êg
thought *n.* nauth
thought, inner *n.* ind
thoughtful *adj.* idhren
thoughtfulness *n.* idhor
thousand, one (1,728) *adj.num.* meneg
thrall *n.* mûl
thread *n.* lain II
thread, fine *n.* lhê
thread, thin *n.* esbin
three *adj.num.* neledh
threshold *n.* fen
throat *n.* lanc II
throne *n.* túrcham
through I *pref.* tre-
through II *prep.* trî
through (together) *adv.* godref
thrust *v.* nasta-
thumb *n.* nawb
thunder *v.* hunna-
tide, high *n.* duinen
tide, low *n.* dannen
tidings *n.* siniath
tidy *adj.* puig
tie *v.* nod-, taetha-
tight (of strings) *adj.* tong
tilted *adj.* adlann
time *n.* lû
tiny *adj.* mîw, pigen, tithen
tire *v.* drautha-
tissue *n.* lann
to *prep.* na
to, for *prep.* an
today *adv.* sír
together *pref.* go-
toil *v.* muda-
tomb *n.* haudh

tomorrow *n.* abarad

tongue, physical *n.* lam I

tool *n.* carf

tooth *n.* carch, nagol, nêl

top *n.* caw

torment *n.* baul

torrent *n.* oll, thórod

tough *adj.* dorn, tara, tarch

toughness *n.* tarias

tower *n.* barad II, minas

tower (up) *v.* brasta-

town, walled *n.* gobel, ost

track *n.* bâd, râd

trade *v.* banga-

traitor *n.* gurgof

trample *v.* batha-

trap *n.* gadas

travel *v.* ledh-

traverse *v.* athrada-, trevad-

treaty *n.* gowest

tree *n.* orn

tree, golden *n.* mallorn

tree, large *n.* galadh

tree, of black wood *n.* lebethron

tree, with a spirit or heart *n.* huorn

tree-woven *adj.* galadhremmen

tress *n.* esbin

tressure *n.* cathrae

triangle *n.* nelthil

triumph *n.* gell

triumphant *adj.* gellui

Troll *n.* torog

troth *n.* gwaedh

trouble *v.* presta-, trasta-

true *adj.* thand II

true-silver *n.* mithril

trumpet *n.* rom

trust I *n.* estel

trust II *v.* estelia-

trusty *adj.* sador, tolog

truth *n.* thannas

try *v.* def-

Tulkas *n.* enner

tune *n.* lind
tuneful *adj.* lend II
tunefully *adv.* lendren
tunic *n.* laub
tunnel *n.* groth
turf *n.* sâdh
turn (into) *v.* ola-
twelve *adj.num.* imp
twilight *n.* tinnu, uial
twin *n.* gwanunig
twine *v.* rig-
twins *n. pl.* gwenyn
twins, pair of *n.* gwanûn, gwanur
twirl *v.* hwinia-
twirling *adj.* hwind
twisted *adj.* norn
twitch I *n.* rinc
twitch II *v.* ritha-
two *adj.num.* tâd
two-legged (animal) *n.* tad-dal
tyrannous *adj.* baug
tyrant *n.* bauglir

ugly *pref.* ul-
Ulmo *n.* ulu
unbreakable *adj.* úragui
under I *pref.* di-
under II *prep.* nu
understand *v.* henia-
undo *v.* dangar-
unintelligence *n.* úchannas
unique *adj.* minai
unite *v.* ertha-
unlovable *adj.* úvelui
unloving *adj.* úvel
unpronounceable *adj.* penbed
unquenchable *adj.* uluithiad
unspeakable *adj.* úbedui
untamed *adj.* rhaw I
untruth *n.* úthannas
unwelcome *adj.* rhudol
up, upon *prep.* am
uphill *adv.* ambenn
uplifting *adj.* amchaled
uproar *n.* glam
urge (on) *v.* hortha-, huia-
Ursa Major *n.* balagerch
us *pron.* men I
use *v.* iuitha-
useful *adj.* maer
usefulness *n.* maeras

vague *adj.* hethu
Vala *n.* balan
vale, deep *n.* im II
Valinor *n.* dor-rodyn
valley *n.* lad
valley, deep or narrow *n.* imlad
valley, deep under/among hills *n.* tum
valley, long and narrow with a watercourse *n.* imrath
valley, of flowers m. imloth
valley, wide *n.* talath
valour *n.* caun II
value *v.* idra-
Vána *n.* banwen
Vanyar *n.* miniel
Varda *n.* elbereth, gilthoniel, fanuilos
vassal *n.* bŷr
vassal, faithful *n.* bôr
vast *adj.* taur III
vastness *n.* tauras
vegetable *n.* pae
veil I *n.* esgal, fân
veil II *v.* fanna-, gwathra-
veiled *adj.* hall II
vein *n.* rant
vengeance *n.* acharn
venom *n.* lhoer
Venus *n.* tanngyl
verse *n.* linnod
very *adv.* íd
victory *n.* tûr
vigilance *n.* tirith
vigour *n.* gorf, hûr
village, walled *n.* gobel
viola *n.* salfin
violence *n.* breged
violent *adj.* asgar, bregol
violet *n.* helinil
violin *n.* salfinnel
virgin *n.* gwend
virginity *n.* gweneth
viscous *adj.* hîw

vision *n.* fanwos
voice *n.* glim
voices, echoing *n.* lamath
voices, many *n.* conath
void *adj.* cofen, gaw, iâ
vomit *v.* pama-
vowel *n.* panna

wagon *n.* rasg I
wait *v.* dar-, dartha-
walk *v.* padra-
wall *n.* ram
wall, great *n.* rammas
wanderer *n.* randir
wandering *n.* mist
wandering, erratic *n.* rain II
want *v.* aníra-
war *n.* auth
ward *v.* tiria-
warlike *n.* authren
warm *adj.* laug
warn *v.* gor-
warrior *n.* maethor
warrior, of orcs *n.* daug
wash *v.* puiga-
watch I *v.* tir-, tiria-
watch II *n.* tirith
watch (from afar) *v.* palandir-
watcher *n.* tirn
water *n.* nen
water, drop of *n.* nenig
water, quiet *n.* lorn
waterfall *n.* lanthir
water-vessel *n.* calph
watery *adj.* nend, nîn III
wave, large *n.* faloth
way *n.* men II, pâd
weapon *n.* carf
weary I *v.* drautha-
weary II *adj.* lom
weave *v.* nathra-
weaver *n.* nathron
web *n.* gwî, nath
wed *v.* besta-
wedding *n.* best
week (of five days) *n.* lefenar
weep *v.* nínia-
weighty *adj.* grond
welcome *v.* nathla-
well I *adv.* al- II (arch.), mae

well II *n.* eithel
werewolf *n.* gaur
west *n.* annûn, dûn
western *adj.* annui
Westron, language of *n.* annúnaid
wet *adj.* limp, mesg, nîd, nîn III
what *interrogative.pron.* man
when I *conj.* ir
when II *interrogative.pron.* mar
where I *conj.* ias
where II *interrogative.pron.* mas
while *conj.* ir
whine *v.* muia-
whirl *v.* hwinia-
whirling *adj.* hwind, hwiniol
whisper I *n.* lhoss, rhoss
whisper II *v.* lhussa-
whistle *v.* sibtha-
white *adj.* faen, fain, nimp I
white, as snow *adj.* uilos
white, shining *adj.* glân I
white-hot *adj.* brassen
whiten *v.* nimmida-
whoever *relative pron.* pephen
wholesome *adj.* alu
why *interrogative.pron.* amman
wicked *adj.* ogol
wide *n.* land II, pann, ûr II
wife *n.* bess, hervess
wield *v.* tortha-
wild *adj.* braig, rhaw I
wilderness *n.* rhovan
will *n.* innas
willow, of *adj.* tathren
willow-tree *n.* tathar
wily *adj.* coru, crumguru
wind (that can be heard) *n.* sûl I
wind (that can be seen) *n.* gwaew
window *n.* henneth
windy *adj.* gwaeren
wine *n.* limp II
wing *n.* rafn
wing, great *n.* roval

winter *n.* rhîw

wisdom *n.* saelas

wise *adj.* goll, golwen, idhren, noen, sael

wish I *n.* iest

wish II *v.* iesta-

without *prep.pref.* pen- I

wizard *n.* curunír, ithron

with, by *prep.* adh

with, by *adv. pref.* an

withered *adj.* tharn

withering *n.* peleth, pelin

woe *n.* naeth

wolf *n.* draug, garaf

wolf-howl *n.* gaul

wolf-men *n.class.pl.* gaurwaith

woman *n.* bess, dî

woman, mortal *n.* firieth

woman, of the race of Man *n.* adaneth

womb *n.* mûn

wondrous *n.* elvennui

wood I *n.* eryn, glad

wood II (as a material) *n.* tawar

wood, great *n.* taur II

wooden *adj.* tawaren

woodpecker *n.* tavor

wool *n.* taw

woolen *adj.* taw

word *n.* peth

word, of good omen *n.* albeth

world *n.* ardhon

worm *n.* leweg

worn (decrepit, of things) *adj.* gern

Wose *n.* drû, drúadan

wound I *v.* harna-

wound II *n.* haru, naedh

wounded *adj.* harn II

woven *adj.* remmen

wreath *n.* rî

wreathe *v.* rig-

wright *n.* tân

wrist *n.* molif

write *v.* teitha-

wrong I *v.* neitha-

wrong II *adj.* raeg
wronged *adj.* neithan

Y

yard *n.* sant
Yavanna *n.* ivann
yawn *v.* iag-
year *n.* idhrinn, în II
year, Valian *n.* ennin
yellow *adj.* malen
yellow-hammer *n.* emlin
yes *affirmation* athon
yesterday *n.* gîr
yet *prep.* dan
yoke *n.* ianu
young *adj.* neth I
youth *n.* nîth I
Yule *n.* durufuin

Z

zebra *n.* rêbroch

Doriathrin Sindarin

A

a *genitive ending* (Dagnir Glaurunga)
al- *pref.* negative, no, not
ar *pref.* outside
Argad *name.* 'outside the fence'
Argador *name.* 'lands outside the fence'

C

cwindor (pindor?) *n.* narrator (a cw becomes a p very early on in Eldarin so this word should perhaps be normalised to pindor)

D

dag- *v.* to slay
dagnir *n.* slayer
dair *n.* shadow of trees
dalf *n.* palm of the hand
Dairon *name*
daudh *n.* pit
Denithor *name* 'lithe and lank'
Dior *name* 'successor'
Dolmed *name* 'wet head'
dôn *n.* back
dor *n.* land
dorn *n.* oak
drôg *n.* wolf
dunn *adj.* dark
dur *n.* dark
durgul *n.* sorcery

E

Eglador *name* Land of the elves
el *n.* star
Elboron *name* 'star fast'
Eld *pl.* **Eldin** *n.* Elf

G

gad *n.* fence
galbreth *n.* beech-tree
gald *n.* tree

ganu *adj.* male
garm *n.* wolf
garth *n.* realm
Garthurian *name* 'fenced realm'
gell *n.* sky
gelu *adj.* blue, sky-blue
(n)gôl *adj.* wise, magical
(n)gold *n.* Noldo
Goldamir *n.* Silmaril (Noldo jewel)
(n)golo *n.* magic
(n)gorth *n.* horror
(n)gorthin *adj.* horrible

H

hedhu *adj.* foggy, obscure, vague

I

-ion *genitive plural ending*

ídhra- *v.* to desire
istel/istil *n.* starlight, silver light

L

lal- *v.* to laugh
laur *n.* gold
líw *n.* fish
lóm *n.* echo
lómen *adj.* echoing
lost *adj.* empty
luin *adj.* blue
lung *adj.* heavy
luth *n.* spell
Luthien *name* 'enchantress'

M

mab *n.* hand
Mablost *name* 'empty hand'
Mablung *name* 'heavy hand'
méd *adj.* wet
meneg *adj.num.card.* thousand
Menegroth *name* 'thousand caves'
míd *n.* moisture

mir/mîr *n.* jewel
morgul/morngul *n.* dark lore, sorcery
morn *adj.* black, dark
moth *n.* pool
muil *n.* twilight, shadow
muilë *n.* secrecy
muilin *adj.* veiled

N

Nan Dungorthin *name* 'vale of black horror'
nand *n.* field, valley
nass *n.* web
Nauglamîr *name* 'necklace of the dwarves'
naugol *n.* dwarf
neld *num.card.* three
neldor *n.* beech
Neldoreth *name,* great beech of Thingol
nivon *n.* forward, west
Nivrim *name* 'west march'
Nivrost *name* 'west vale'
nîw *n.* nose

O

orn *n.* tree, high tree
orth *pl.* **orthin** *n.* mountain

R

radhon *n.* east
Radhrim *name* 'east march'
Radhrost *name* 'east vale'
Region *name* 'hollin'
regorn *pl.* **regin** *n.* holly-tree
rim *n.* edge, hem, border
ring *n.* cold pool, or lake in mountains
rost *n.* plain, wide land (between mountains)
rodh/roth *pl.* **rodhin** *n.* cave

T

Thingol *name* 'grey cloak'
Thurin *name* 'secret'
Thuringwethil *name* 'secret shadow'

U

umboth *n.* large pool
urch *pl.* **urchin** *n.* orc